Best Easy Day Hikes
Fresno

Help Us Keep This Guide Up to Date

Every effort has been made by the author and editors to make this guide as accurate and useful as possible. However, many things can change after a guide is published—trails are rerouted, regulations change, facilities come under new management, etc.

We would appreciate hearing from you concerning your experiences with this guide and how you feel it could be improved and kept up to date. While we may not be able to respond to all comments and suggestions, we'll take them to heart and we'll also make certain to share them with the author. Please send your comments and suggestions to the following address:

> GPP
> Reader Response/Editorial Department
> P.O. Box 480
> Guilford, CT 06437

Or you may e-mail us at:

> editorial@GlobePequot.com

Thanks for your input, and happy trails!

Best Easy Day Hikes Series

Best Easy Day Hikes
Fresno

Tracy Salcedo-Chourré

FALCONGUIDES

GUILFORD, CONNECTICUT
HELENA, MONTANA

AN IMPRINT OF THE GLOBE PEQUOT PRESS

FALCONGUIDES®

Copyright © 2012 by Morris Book Publishing, LLC

ALL RIGHTS RESERVED. No part of this book may be reproduced
or transmitted in any form by any means, electronic or mechanical,
including photocopying and recording, or by any information storage
and retrieval system, except as may be expressly permitted in writing
from the publisher. Requests for permission should be addressed to
Globe Pequot Press, Attn: Rights and Permissions Department, P.O.
Box 480, Guilford CT 06437.

FalconGuides is an imprint of Globe Pequot Press.
Falcon, FalconGuides, and Outfit Your Mind are registered trademarks
of Morris Book Publishing, LLC.

Maps by Mapping Specialists Ltd. © Morris Book Publishing, LLC
TOPO! Explorer software and SuperQuad source maps courtesy of
National Geographic Maps. For information about TOPO! Explorer,
TOPO!, and Nat Geo Maps products, go to www.topo.com or www
.natgeomaps.com.

Project editor: Julie Marsh
Layout: Joanna Beyer

Library of Congress Cataloging-in-Publication Data is available on file.
ISBN 978-0-7627-7280-3

Printed in the United States of America
10 9 8 7 6 5 4 3 2 1

Contents

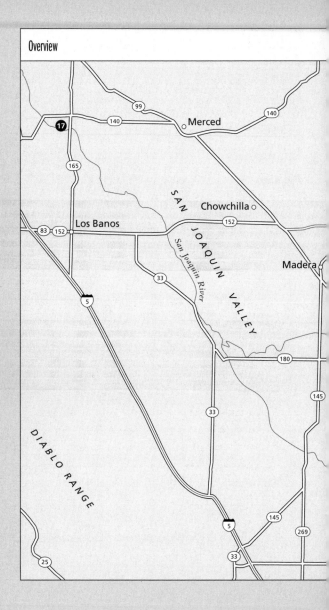

Acknowledgments

Thanks to these organizations for their preservation efforts and review of hike descriptions for accuracy: the Sierra National Forest, the US Army Corps of Engineers, the city and county of Fresno, the San Joaquin River Parkway and Conservation Trust, the San Luis National Wildlife Refuge, and the Sequoia Riverlands Trust.

Because much of this terrain was new to me, I relied heavily on the advice of fellow hikers to find the best hikes around Fresno. Thanks to docents Mike Mirigan and Frank and Jane Campbell, as well as all the friendly hikers that I met on the trail, for their tips. I only wish the grouchy winter weather had allowed me to explore more!

Thanks to the expert editors, layout artists, mapmakers, and proofreaders at FalconGuides and Globe Pequot Press for making this guide the best it can be.

Most of all, thanks to my sons Jesse, Cruz, and Penn, and my husband, Martin.

Introduction

I've got to say, when I told people I was compiling a guide to the best easy day hikes in Fresno, I was met with skepticism. Fresno? Hiking? This is a town better known to outsiders as the center of California's farmland region—you don't hike in Fresno, you buy oranges and strawberries here.

But as is so often the case, the stereotype doesn't match the reality. Fresno has much to offer in the way of great hiking trails, from a growing set of popular urban pathways to amazingly scenic treks in the foothills of the Sierra Nevada.

The mighty San Joaquin River system informs the region. Trails follow its banks, wind through towns that grew up along its course, wander around reservoirs built on it and its tributaries, and explore the foothills of the mountains in which it originates. The will and whimsy of the San Joaquin, which historically frequently spilled over its banks, flooding towns like Millerton into eventual oblivion, is these days contained with a system of levees, canals, sloughs, and dams. The harnessing of the river has been a boon to development in the valley, from watering California's breadbasket crops to providing power for the people who cultivate those crops. Hiking plays second fiddle to agriculture along the San Joaquin, but as the population grows, so too will the need and desire to preserve the valley's open spaces and provide trail access.

As the gateway to Yosemite, it's difficult to think of Fresno and the San Joaquin Valley without thinking about pioneering naturalist John Muir. In *The Mountains of California,* he writes about carpets of wildflowers—"one sheet of purple and gold"—spread across the valley floor. Though not nearly as expansive, a springtime hike on the flatlands may lead you into a patch of color that evokes the bounty Muir described. That's the promise of hiking in Fresno.

The Nature of Fresno

Trails in Fresno and the neighboring foothills of the Sierra Nevada range from rough and hilly to flat and paved. Hikes in this guide cover the gamut. While by definition a "best easy day hike" poses little danger to the traveler, knowing a few details about the nature of the region will enhance your explorations.

Weather

Fresno's weather is, for the most part, temperate. But extremes of winter in the higher elevations (snow, cold) and summer on the flatlands (heat, sun, and air pollution) may preclude comfortable hiking in certain months.

There are essentially two seasons in Fresno: the rainy and the dry. The rainy season runs from November to March and typical daytime highs range from the mid-40s to the mid-60s Fahrenheit. Rains are periodically heavy, and snow blankets trails in the foothills of the Sierra. The valley also may be blanketed in dense fog, most commonly in December, January, and February, which obscures all vistas and makes driving difficult.

The dry season runs from April to October, with average daily temperatures ranging from the 60s to the 80s F. Temperatures may skyrocket into the 100s between June and September. Heat, sunlight, and chemicals from auto emissions and other factors combine in summer to create unhealthy ozone levels in the air. When an air quality advisory is issued, avoid hiking.

Spring and fall, when temperatures moderate and there is less chance of access being limited by weather extremes and air quality, are the best hiking seasons. Always be prepared for changeable weather—rain, cold, or heat—by wearing layers and packing waterproof gear.

Potential Hazards

While the only critters you're likely to encounter on the trail are butterflies and bunnies, there is the chance you may run across an animal with the potential to cause harm.

Rattlesnakes are found throughout the region and are active primarily in the late spring, summer, and fall. Signs at trailheads alert hikers if rattlesnakes are present, and some identify other, nonvenomous snakes that share the habitat. Rattlesnakes generally only strike if they are threatened. Keep your distance and they will keep theirs. Snakes generally take shelter from the scorching sun at midday. Scan the trail ahead, and be sure to look before you place your hands or feet on rocks or behind logs.

Encounters with mountain lions are unlikely but possible. Signs at trailheads warn hikers if these animals might be present. If you encounter a mountain lion, make yourself as big as possible and do not run. If you don't act like or look like prey, you stand a good chance of not being attacked.

Several varieties of insects may pester hikers. Ticks are potential vectors of Lyme disease. Wear light-colored, long-sleeved shirts and trousers so that you can see the bugs. Remove any ticks that attach as quickly as possible, and seek medical treatment if a rash or illness occurs after a tick bite. Wear insect repellent to ward off mosquitoes and biting flies. Yellow jackets also pose a hazard, primarily around reservoirs where they find food in trash and picnics. If you are allergic, carry medication.

Poison oak (leaves of three, let it be) can cause a nasty, long-lasting skin irritation. It grows both along flatland trails (particularly along riversides) and in the foothills. Avoid contact with the plant by staying on formal trails.

Swimming in rivers and reservoirs may be possible at certain times of year and in certain locations. Be sure to contact the land manager of the lake or stream you'd like to swim in before taking a dip. Because the San Joaquin and its tributaries are dammed at numerous locations, water levels and flows may fluctuate without warning. Do not swim in canals or flumes, as the water moves deceptively fast.

Be Prepared

Hikers should be prepared for any situation, whether they are out for a short stroll through Woodward Park or hiking up Lewis Creek. Some specific advice:

- Know the basics of first aid, including how to treat bleeding; bites and stings; and fractures, strains, or sprains. Pack a first-aid kit on any excursion.
- Know the symptoms of both cold- and heat-related conditions, including hypothermia and heat stroke. The best way to avoid these afflictions is to wear appropriate clothing, drink lots of water, eat enough to keep the internal fires properly stoked, and keep a pace that is within your physical limits.
- Regardless of the weather, your body needs a lot of water while hiking. Drinking a full thirty-two-ounce bottle on each outing is a good idea no matter how short the hike. More is better.

- Don't drink from rivers, creeks, or lakes without treating or filtering the water first. Untreated water may host a variety of contaminants, including *Giardia*, which can cause serious intestinal unrest.

- Wear sunscreen.

- Carry a backpack in which you can store extra clothing; drinking water and food; and goodies like guidebooks, a camera, and binoculars.

- Many trails have cell phone coverage. Bring your device, but make sure it's turned off or on the vibrate setting.

- Watch children carefully. Waterways move deceptively fast, animals and plants may harbor danger, and rocky terrain and cliffs are potential hazards. Children should carry a plastic whistle; if they become lost, they should stay in one place and blow the whistle to summon help.

Leave No Trace

Trails in the Fresno area, particularly in the foothills and around reservoirs, are heavily used year-round. We, as trail users and advocates, must be especially vigilant to make sure our passage leaves no lasting mark. Here are some basic guidelines for preserving trails in the region:

- Pack out all trash, including biodegradable items like apple cores. You might also pack out garbage left by less considerate hikers.

- Avoid damaging fragile soils and plants by remaining on established routes and not cutting switchbacks. Social trails contribute to erosion problems and create unsightly scars on the landscape.

- Don't approach or feed any wild creatures—they are best able to survive if they remain self-reliant.

- Don't pick wildflowers or gather rocks, antlers, feathers, and other treasures along the trail. Removing these items will only take away from the next hiker's experience.

- Be courteous by not making loud noises while hiking.

- Many of these trails are multiuse, which means you'll share them with other hikers, trail runners, mountain bikers, and equestrians. Familiarize yourself with proper trail etiquette, yielding the trail when appropriate. If you are hiking with a group, walk single file when passing other hikers.

- Use outhouses at trailheads or along the trail.

- For more information visit www.LNT.org.

Getting Around

Most hikes in this guide are within an hour's drive of downtown Fresno. A few are a bit farther out but are included because they offer a taste of the country that informs the ecology and environment of the greater San Joaquin Valley. Directions to each trailhead are given from the nearest major city or town, beginning from the nearest major highway.

Major thoroughfares in the Fresno area include CA 99 (north–south), CA 41 (north–south), and CA 168 (east–west). The other major Central Valley highway, I-5, is located about an hour's drive west of the city.

Public transportation generally doesn't run to these out-of-the-way trailheads. However, if you are interested in using public transit to get as close as possible to your final destination, contact Fresno Area Express (FAX) at (559) 621-RIDE (7433) or www.fresno.gov/DiscoverFresno/ PublicTransportation/default.htm.

Land Management

The following government agencies manage public lands described in this guide and can provide further information on other trails and parks in their service areas.

- **California State Parks** at www.parks.ca.gov; select a park and its site will download. Contact information for state parks in this guide is provided in the specifications at the beginning of each hike description.
- **Sierra National Forest,** 1600 Tollhouse Rd., Clovis, CA 93611; (559) 297-0706; www.fs.fed.us/r5/sierra
- **Bass Lake Ranger District** (Sierra National Forest), 57003 Road 225, North Fork, CA 93643; (559) 877-2218; www.fs.fed.us/r5/sierra
- **High Sierra Ranger District** (Sierra National Forest), 29688 Auberry Rd./P.O. Box 559, Prather, CA 93651; (559) 855-5355; www.fs.fed.us/r5/sierra
- **San Joaquin River Parkway and Conservation Trust,** 11605 Old Friant Rd., Fresno, CA 93730; (559) 248-8480; www.riverparkway.org
- **National Park Service** at www.nps.gov; select a state or park and its site will download. While none of the hikes in this guide are in national parks proper, both Yosemite National Park and Sequoia and Kings Canyon National Parks are nearby.

How to Use This Guide

This book is designed to be simple and easy to use. Each hike is described with a map and summary information that delivers the trail's vital statistics including length, difficulty, fees and permits, park hours, canine compatibility, and trail contacts. Directions to the trailhead are provided. Information about what you'll see along each trail, as well as tidbits about the natural and cultural history, are included in hike descriptions. A detailed route finder (Miles and Directions) sets forth mileages between significant landmarks.

How the Hikes Were Chosen

Hikes range in difficulty from flat excursions to more challenging treks into the foothills. I've selected hikes that will take no more than one and a half to two hours to reach. Longer drives are required to reach hikes in the foothills, a cool option on hot summer days or when air quality is poor. Hikes were selected to showcase both the flatland and mountainous aspects of the Fresno area.

While these trails are among the best, keep in mind that nearby trails may offer options better suited to your needs. In addition, traveling farther into the foothills will enable you to explore trails at Shaver Lake and Huntington Lake, and in Yosemite and Sequoia and Kings Canyon National Parks. This guide does not include hikes at Shaver Lake, Huntington Lake, and other reservoirs in the foothills east of Fresno due to excessive snowfall in the winter of 2010–2011, which precluded on-the-ground research. Potential alternatives are suggested in the Options sections at the end of some hike descriptions.

Selecting a Hike

These are all easy hikes, but easy is a relative term. Some would argue that no hike involving any kind of climbing is easy, but in the foothills east of Fresno, hills are a fact of life. To aid in selecting a hike that suits particular needs and abilities, they are rated easy, moderate, and more challenging. Bear in mind that even the most challenging can be made easy by hiking within your limits and taking rests when you need them.

- **Easy** hikes are generally short and flat, taking no longer than an hour to complete.
- **Moderate** hikes involve increased distance and changes in elevation, and take one to two hours to complete.
- **More challenging** hikes feature some steep stretches and generally take longer than two hours to complete.

What you think is easy is entirely dependent on your level of fitness and the adequacy of your gear (primarily shoes). Use the trail's length as a gauge of its relative difficulty—even if climbing is involved, it won't be bad if the hike is less than 1 mile long. If you are hiking with a group, select a hike that's appropriate for the least fit and prepared in your party.

Approximate hiking times are based on the assumption that on flat ground, most walkers average 2 miles per hour. Adjust that rate by the steepness of the terrain and your level of fitness (subtract time if you're an aerobic animal and add time if you're hiking with kids). Be sure to add more time if you plan to picnic or take part in other activities like bird watching or photography.

Trail Finder

Best Hikes for Dogs

Hike Ratings

(Hikes are listed from easiest to most challenging.)

Map Legend

══99══	State Highway
══222══	Local Road
- - - - - -	Unpaved Road
▬▬▬▬▬▬	Featured Trail
- - - - - - -	Trail
- ·· - ·· - ·· -	County Line
～～～	River/Creek
⬭	Body of Water
▥	Local/State Park
▥	National Park
▬	Bench
⛵	Boat Launch
◡◡	Bridge
⛰	Camping
•—•	Gate
❷	Information Center
▲	Mountain Peak/Elevation
🅿	Parking
⊞	Picnic Area
■	Point of Interest/Structure
🚻	Restroom
○	Town
⓫	Trailhead
🥾	Viewpoint/Overlook
🚰	Water
⩘	Waterfall

1 Hidden Homes Nature Trail

This interpretive path encircles a sweet little pond that's popular with local ducks and families interested in a hands-on encounter with the natural world.

Distance: 0.5-mile loop
Approximate hiking time: 30 to 45 minutes
Difficulty: Easy
Trail surface: Crushed gravel; wheelchair and stroller accessible
Best seasons: Year-round
Other trail users: None
Canine compatibility: Dogs not permitted
Fees and permits: None

Schedule: Open daily year-round from sunrise to sunset; parkway trust facilities open from 8 a.m. to 3 p.m. daily
Trailhead facilities: Ample parking, restrooms, information center and museum
Maps: USGS Lanes Bridge CA
Trail contact: San Joaquin River Parkway and Conservation Trust, 11605 Old Friant Rd., Fresno 93737; (559) 248-8480; www .riverparkway.org

Finding the trailhead: From CA 41 in Fresno, take the Friant Road exit (at the River Park mall). Follow Friant Road 4.3 miles northeast to Old Friant Road, signed and on the left. Follow Old Friant Road for 1.0 mile to the signed turn into the San Joaquin River Parkway Trust/Coke Hallowell Center for River Studies on the left. GPS: N36 54.398'/W119 45.450'

The Hike

Pretend you are a caddis fly larva. What do you look like? Where do you live? You (and your children) can find out on the Hidden Homes Nature Trail, which circumnavigates a small pond adjacent to the headquarters of the San Joaquin River Parkway and Conservation Trust and the historic Riverview Ranch house.

On this easy interpretive trail, perfect for families with young children, you also can venture into the mock homes of great horned owls, salmon, bald eagles, killdeer, and mice. Though the intended audience is youngsters, parents and grandparents will be charmed by the thoughtfully re-created nests and habitats that line the path.

The trail's setting is marshland and grassland in the San Joaquin River floodplain, with a few trees and abundant grasses (and wildflowers in season) encircling the pond. Ducks are frequent visitors to the pond, while great horned owls roost in cavities in the stately palms that line the entry road to the historic ranch.

Begin the short hike at a break in the fence opposite the River Ranch Welcome Pavilion. Described in a counterclockwise direction, begin the loop by heading right at the interpretive sign, passing overlook benches and viewing scopes.

Interpretive displays line the trail, with the first being the great horned owl's roost. Other "homes," like the bald eagle's nest and the mouse tunnel, make this a charming introduction to hiking in the Fresno area.

The paved Lewis S. Eaton Trail parallels the nature path for a stretch as it circles back toward the trailhead, offering the opportunity to extend the hike into neighboring Woodward Park. The multiuse path is popular with runners, cyclists, and hikers.

Take some time, either at the beginning or end of your trip around the Hidden Homes Nature Trail, to tour the Riverview Ranch House. Inside you'll find interpretive

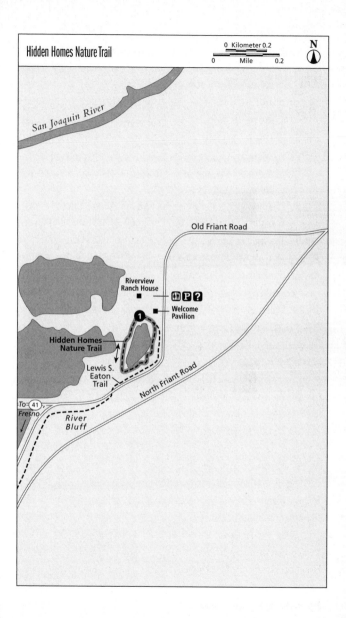

displays, libraries and reading rooms, and viewing rooms. You can enjoy the gardens, vineyard, and verandah as well.

Miles and Directions

0.0 Start opposite the River Ranch Welcome Pavilion, at a break in the fence bordering the pond. Turn right to follow the path in a counterclockwise direction.

0.1 Take the short branch right to the dead-end at the eagle's nest exhibit. Retrace your steps to the main trail and continue to the right around the pond.

0.3 Take the side trail right to the killdeer "scrape" (nest), then backtrack again to the main trail and go right to continue.

0.5 The mouse tunnel is the last exhibit along the trail. Arrive back at the trailhead opposite the welcome pavilion.

2 Lewis S. Eaton Trail

This section of the growing San Joaquin River Parkway trail system traces the top of a bluff overlooking the San Joaquin River and its floodplain. Woodward Park is at the hike's turnaround point, and views of the high Sierra accompany the return.

Distance: 6.5 miles out and back
Approximate hiking time: 3.5 hours
Difficulty: Moderate due to length
Trail surface: Pavement
Best seasons: Year-round
Other trail users: Cyclists, runners, equestrians on cross-trails near Woodward Park
Canine compatibility: Leashed dogs permitted
Fees and permits: None
Schedule: Open daily year-round from sunrise to sunset
Trailhead facilities: Paved parking lot, restrooms, water, information, trashcans. Restrooms, water, trashcans, and other amenities are available along the trail and at the turnaround point in Woodward Park.
Maps: USGS Lanes Bridge CA and Fresno North CA; online at www.fresno.gov/NR/rdon lyres/D092035D-4626-436A -BCB4-4910F53D7514/0/ Trailsmap.pdf
Trail contact: San Joaquin River Parkway and Conservation Trust, 11605 Old Friant Rd., Fresno 93737; (559) 248-8480; www .riverparkway.org

Finding the trailhead: From CA 41 in Fresno, take the Friant Road exit (at the River Park mall). Follow Friant Road 4.3 miles northeast to Old Friant Road, signed and on the left. Follow Old Friant Road for 1.0 mile to the signed turn into the San Joaquin River Parkway Trust/Coke Hallowell Center for River Studies on the left. GPS: N36 54.402'/W119 45.449'

The Hike

Named for Fresno philanthropist Lewis S. Eaton, this paved section of the San Joaquin River Parkway stretches 5 miles from the Coke Hallowell Center for River Studies on Old Friant Road into sprawling Woodward Park. It's popular with runners, cyclists, and walkers from throughout the Fresno area and beyond. With plans to extend the trail for 22 miles, the route is sure to be a major recreational attraction for years to come.

The section of trail described here leads into Fresno's premier city park, where it links to other trails including the Tom MacMichael Sr. Trail in Jensen River Ranch. The path rides a bluff overlooking the San Joaquin River, offering views of the floodplain, the workings of the Vulcan aggregate operation, and out over the lowlands of the Central Valley. On the return trip, above the gentle rise of the foothills, the snowcapped peaks of the Sierra Nevada can be seen.

The trail can be picked up anywhere along its length, but it's described here starting at the conservation trust complex off Old Friant Road. After paralleling the Hidden Homes trail for a short distance, the route climbs out of the bottomlands onto the bluff, which rises as high as 90 feet above the river. A bridge spans Old Friant Road near its junction with Friant Road; from there the path snakes south and west along the bluff top.

Views along the first section of the trail stretch north and west across the workings of the Vulcan Materials Company, which produces construction aggregates like gravel, crushed stone, and sand. Vulcan has been recognized for its environmental friendliness by the Wildlife Habitat Council.

Ponds lined with cattails and reeds, where ducks and other waterfowl and birdlife congregate, exemplify the company's efforts to support and restore habitat.

Leaving the gravel works behind, the viewscape extends over Jensen River Ranch, a parkway trust property that is being restored to its natural state as a valley oak woodland. Interpretive signs along this stretch of the Eaton trail (which also offers shaded benches to sit on while enjoying the views) describe the restoration process and the geologic forces that shaped the bluff and the floodplain below.

The turnaround point is just inside the boundary of Woodward Park, where more interpretive signs inform a rest area with benches and a water fountain. A low stone wall surrounds a circle paved in brick; beyond this the greens, trails, and amenities of Woodward Park can be enjoyed. On the return trip, views open eastward onto the snowy peaks of the high Sierra.

This is very much an urban trail, with neighborhoods and busy Friant Road bordering the route on south. But that doesn't detract from its popularity, and you are destined to share with many other trail users. Fortunately, the Eaton trail is plenty wide enough and long enough to accommodate all users.

Miles and Directions

0.0 Start at the trailhead opposite the welcome pavilion at the Coke Hallowell center. The paved track parallels the Hidden Homes Nature Trail.

0.3 Cross Old Friant Road and head right on the trail, beginning a gentle climb.

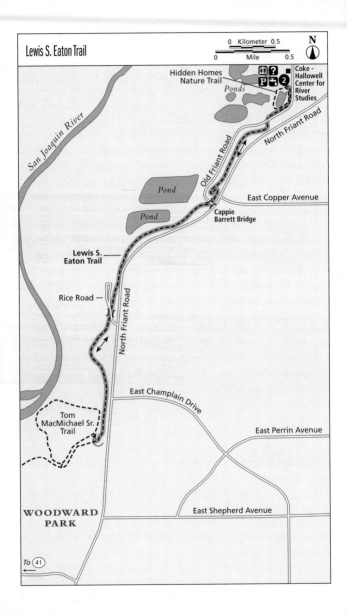

Lewis S. Eaton Trail

San Joaquin River

0   Kilometer   0.5
0   Mile   0.5

N

Hidden Homes
Nature Trail

Ponds

Coke -
Hallowell
Center for
River
Studies

2

North Friant Road

Old Friant Road

Pond

East Copper Avenue

Pond

Cappie
Barrett Bridge

Lewis S.
Eaton Trail

Rice Road

North Friant Road

East Champlain Drive

Tom
MacMichael Sr.
Trail

East Perrin Avenue

WOODWARD
PARK

East Shepherd Avenue

To 41

1.0 Round a sweeping S curve to the top of the bluff. Pass two trail links to and along Friant Road, with memorial plantings and a bench. Stay right and southbound on the Eaton trail.

1.25 Cross the Cappie Barrett Bridge, which spans Old Friant Road. Beyond, a couple of benches offer respite in the shade.

1.75 Pass a rest stop with restrooms, benches, water, and a memorial to Lewis Eaton. An interpretive sign describes how the San Joaquin River carved its present bed from its ancient alluvial fan.

1.9 Pass another set of benches in a small grove of trees.

2.1 Pass yet another bench/grove combo.

2.3 Cross the bridge over Rice Road.

2.6 Pass an interpretive sign that describes the native valley oak woodland that once occupied the bottomlands, which overlooks the Jensen River Ranch. Another set of benches is 0.1 mile beyond.

2.9 Pass Champlain Drive. Horse trails intersect the paved path.

3.25 Enter Woodward Park. Turn around in the brick circle surrounded by a low stone wall, and return as you came.

6.5 Arrive back at the trailhead.

3 Tom MacMichael Sr. Trail (Woodward Park and Jensen River Ranch)

While the wildlands of the Jensen River Ranch are the focal point of this route, the trail also borders Woodward Park's entertaining BMX bike course.

Distance: 3.5-mile lollipop

Approximate hiking time: 2 hours

Difficulty: Easy

Trail surface: Broad packed-dirt path; short section of pavement is handicapped-accessible

Best seasons: Year-round. Standing water may be on the path near the flood control basin and spillway after rain.

Other trail users: Mountain bikers, trail runners, equestrians on linked horse trails

Canine compatibility: Leashed dogs permitted

Fees and permits: A car entry fee is charged for Woodward Park; bicycle and pedestrian traffic is free.

Schedule: Open daily year-round from sunrise to sunset

Trailhead facilities: Large paved parking lot, restrooms, water, bike rack, and picnic facilities. Other facilities are available throughout the park.

Maps: USGS Fresno North CA and Lanes Bridge CA; online at www.fresno.gov/NR/rdonlyres/21023F8C-C8D7-4AE0-9DDE-A789AA446401/3239/WoodwardMap.pdf (does not include the portion of the trail in the Jensen River Ranch parcel)

Trail contacts: City of Fresno, 1515 E. Divisadero, Fresno 93721; (559) 621-2900; www.fresno.gov/Government/DepartmentDirectory/Parksand Recreation/ParksandFacilities/Regional+Parks/WoodwardPark .htm. San Joaquin River Parkway and Conservation Trust, 11605 Old Friant Rd., Fresno 93737; (559) 248-8480; www.riverpark way.org

Finding the trailhead: From CA 41, take the Friant Road exit. Head northeast on Friant Road for 1.3 miles to the signed left turn into Woodward Park. Proceed to the entrance station and pay the fee, then continue 0.1 mile on the park road (Yosemite Road) to a junction. Turn right and drive 1.1 miles to the signed Sunset View parking area on the left. Park in the lot; the broad unsigned trail is located just across the park road, reached via any of several social paths. GPS: N36 51.743' / W119 47.406'

The Hike

There's a lot to recommend Woodward Park. Hailed as the largest park of its kind in the Central Valley, the 325-acre facility encompasses picnic shelters, fishing ponds, playing greens, tot lots, a dog park, a disc golf course, a par course, an amphitheater, a BMX cycling venue—and a wonderful day hike lollipop.

Established as a bequest from Fresno philanthropist Ralph Woodward, who wished this portion of his estate to be preserved as parkland and a bird sanctuary, the park is a hub for Fresno outdoors people. Hikers and walkers enjoy a section of the paved Lewis S. Eaton Trail, which will eventually reach 22 miles from Friant Dam into the city, as well as horse trails and other paths. With the addition of the riverfront parcel at Jensen River Ranch, once a hog farm and undergoing reclamation, the park is also a gateway to a wonderful natural habitat. The Jensen ranch property, managed by the San Joaquin River Parkway and Conservation Trust, serves as habitat for local wildlife, notably ground squirrels and the raptors that hunt them.

Despite the ongoing rehabilitation effort on the ranch, this is by no means a wilderness trek. The route runs through the BMX course at its beginning and end—the cyclists are a ton of fun to watch. Road noise from nearby CA 41 is muffled by a brick sound barrier and fades on the reclaimed ranch. A steep spillway drops down the hillside into the ranch property at the far end of the loop, channeling drainage from a neighborhood bordering the park. Most vistas encompass homes or other man-made structures. But don't be put off: It is the perfect outing for families, an evening stroll, or an early morning workout.

Begin on a broad dirt multiuse track bordered by grass and the highway's sound barrier. The walk-and-talk trail heads easily uphill to the BMX cycling area, with a rollercoaster bike track on the left and a competitive course with bleachers on the right. Several unmarked trails that link to the main paved park road intersect as you proceed, but the main trail is obvious. At the top of the gentle climb, you'll leave the cyclists behind, dropping down to the paved Lewis S. Eaton Trail, then onto the dirt Tom MacMichael Sr. Trail.

Circling the meadow in the bottomlands on the MacMichael trail brings you first to the banks of the San Joaquin River, where there are picnic tables and restrooms. Riparian plants grow thickly along its course; in the meadowland to the right, young trees, including the native valley oak, have been planted as part of the restoration project. Watch for birds flying overhead and foraging in the scrub, and ground squirrels and gophers scurrying through the grass. These burrowing critters were responsible for the failure of canals built by rancher Moses Church in an effort to irrigate his crops and provide green range for his livestock. Their tunnels undermined the construction, and the canals collapsed.

At the broad flood-control detention basin, which supports an artificial riparian zone that stays green into the dry season, the trail turns sharply east (right). At the stormwater energy dissipater (which resembles the spillway of a dam), the route again turns sharply right, now to the south, and runs along the bottom of the steep bluff. The bluff wall is pocked with burrows of ground squirrels, and hawks circle overhead or watch from perches in the willows and scraggly cottonwoods along the streamlet to the right.

Close the loop at the entrance to the Jensen ranch and retrace your steps to the trailhead.

Miles and Directions

0.0 Start by crossing the park road and heading right on the multiuse dirt trail.

0.2 Stay left on the obvious track at the junction with a trail leading right to the park's fishing pond.

0.3 Stay left at the junction with a trail that links to the park road.

0.4 Pass a gate and a sign that marks a horse trail. BMX facilities line both sides of the trail, and the disc golf course borders the trail on the right. Pass a pond, staying on the trail that borders the fence line.

0.7 Cross the BMX trail. Views drop down into the bottomlands and the track is wedged between two fences. Stay left at the unmarked trail junction at the end of the BMX course, passing a viewing bench.

1.0 A brief steep descent leads to a gate and a couple of trail intersections. Go left on the main trail, then left again, across the paved Eaton trail, into the Jensen River Ranch tract. The loop portion of the route is described in a clockwise direction. Head left, past the information sign, on the signed MacMichael trail.

1.1 At the junction with the signed equestrian trail, stay right on the unsigned MacMichael trail.

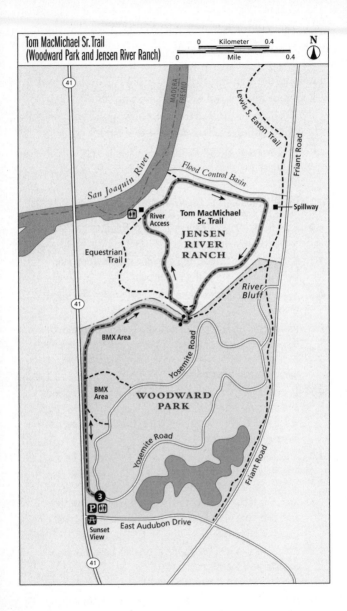

1.4 Arrive at the riverbank. There are picnic facilities, water, restrooms, and a signboard at this point. The equestrian trail rejoins the MacMichael trail. Continue north, passing a utility building.

1.7 At the flood-control slough, turn right on the loop trail. A secondary trail leads right toward the river.

2.0 At the base of the storm water spillway, the trail turns sharply right.

2.5 Close the MacMichael loop at the junction, and head uphill to pick up the path through the BMX area. Retrace your steps.

3.5 Arrive back at the trailhead.

4 Fresno Sugar Pine Trail

This section of a regional rail trail leads from River Park's shops and eateries into suburban Fresno, with the turnaround at a neighborhood park.

Distance: 5.2 miles out and back

Approximate hiking time: 2.5 hours

Difficulty: Moderate due to trail length

Trail surface: Pavement

Best seasons: Year-round

Other trail users: Cyclists, runners

Canine compatibility: Leashed dogs permitted

Fees and permits: None

Schedule: Open daily year-round from sunrise to sunset

Trailhead facilities: Benches and trashcans at the trailhead proper. Restrooms, parking, water, and shopping/dining outlets are available at the River Park mall.

Maps: USGS Fresno North CA and Clovis CA; online at www .fresno.gov/NR/rdonlyres/ D092035D-4626-436A -BCB4-4910F53D7514/0/ Trailsmap.pdf

Trail contact: Fresno City Parks and Recreation Department, 1515 E. Divisadero, Fresno 93721; (559) 621-2900; www .fresno.gov

Finding the trailhead: From CA 41 in Fresno, take the Friant Road exit. Head southwest on Friant Road for 1 block to its intersection with Nees Avenue. Go left (west) on Nees Avenue for less than 1 block to the entrance to the covered parking lot at River Park mall. Pull into the covered lot and park. The trailhead is across Nees Avenue from the mall lot under the freeway overpass; use the signalized crosswalk at La Entrada to access. GPS: N36 51.078'/ W119 47.343'

The Hike

Thousands of trees that were planted in 2000 have begun to mature, making the Fresno Sugar Pine Trail (and its linked Clovis Old Town Trails) a shady—and lovely—urban rail trail.

At 13 miles one way, the Sugar Pine/Old Town route is too long to qualify as an easy hike, but this section, which runs from the River Park mall to a neighborhood park at the intersection of Maple and Shepherd Avenues, exemplifies what a rail trail (or any urban trail for that matter) does best. It links neighborhoods to schools, workplaces, retail outlets, and community parks, and provides peaceful stretches of uninterrupted pathway for hikers, runners, cyclists, and dog walkers.

The route follows the Clovis Branchline/Pinedale Spur railroad corridor through northern Fresno and Old Town Clovis. The abandoned grade was purchased by the two cities from Union Pacific in 1997, and the rail trail is the product of a concerted community effort spearheaded by the Coalition for Community Trails, in cooperation with other nonprofit and public agencies.

In a remarkable feat that sets this trail apart from any other in the world, thirty-three different varieties of trees were planted in the spring of 2000—"4,400 trees planted by 3,000 volunteers setting a Guinness World Record," according to the trail website. Though by no means a wilderness walk, the trees go a long way toward beautifying both the route and the surrounding community.

Following the trail is simple. After an inauspicious beginning under a freeway overpass, the trail rolls into a nice suburban neighborhood. The finest section is sandwiched in a

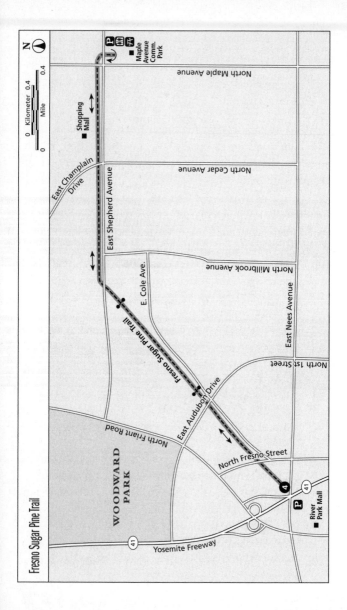

Fresno Sugar Pine Trail

greenbelt lined with evergreens, with the backyard fences of local homes lending the trail some privacy. The snowcapped peaks of the Sierra are visible ahead.

At the route's intersection with Shepherd Avenue, the trail becomes distinctly citified. It borders the busy thoroughfare, passing a shopping mall and some apartment complexes, leading to Maple Avenue. Cross Shepherd Avenue and take a breather in the little community park on the corner of Maple and Shepherd, with a tot lot, restrooms, playing greens, and picnic facilities. Retrace your steps to the trailhead.

Miles and Directions

0.0 Start by leaving the parking garage. Follow the sidewalk beside Nees Avenue east to the traffic signal and crosswalk. Cross the road and pick up the signed Fresno Sugar Pine Trail under the overpass.

0.2 A lighted tunnel takes the trail under Fresno Street.

0.3 Leave office complexes behind as you enter a quiet neighborhood, with Cole Avenue running alongside on the right and an open field on the left.

0.6 Cross Audubon Drive and pass a gate. The trail is a straight shot toward the mountains, shaded by evergreens. You can hear dogs barking and children playing behind the backyard privacy fences.

1.4 Pass a second gate to the Shepherd Avenue intersection. A crosswalk fosters passage across the four-lane roadway. If you'd rather have a signal, head right to the arterial at Millbrook Avenue.

2.0 Cross Champlain Drive. A shopping mall and apartment complexes line the trail beyond.

2.6 Arrive at Maple Avenue. Cross Shepherd to the park, rest and refresh, then retrace your steps to the trailhead.

5.1 Arrive back at the trailhead. Cross Nees Avenue to return to the parking area.

5.2 Arrive back at the parking area.

5 Lost Lake Nature Trail

The rich riparian zone that thrives on the banks of the San Joaquin River provides the setting for a trail on Fresno's urban boundary. Watch and listen for golden eagles in the treetops.

Distance: 1.2 miles out and back

Approximate hiking time: 1 hour

Difficulty: Easy

Trail surface: Sand, dirt single-track, cobbled creek bed, dirt roadway

Best seasons: Late spring, summer, fall

Other trail users: Mountain bikers, anglers

Canine compatibility: Leashed dogs permitted

Fees and permits: A day-use fee is charged

Schedule: Open daily from 5 a.m. to 10 p.m. Apr to Oct; from 5 a.m. to 7 p.m. Nov to Mar

Trailhead facilities: Small parking lot, trashcans, and an information signboard at the trailhead; picnic facilities and restrooms are located throughout the riverfront activity area.

Maps: USGS Friant CA

Trail contact: Fresno County Department of Public Works and Planning Resources and Parks Division, 2220 Tulare St., 6th floor, Fresno 93721; (559) 488-3004; www.co.fresno.ca.us

Finding the trailhead: From downtown Fresno, follow CA 41 north to the Friant Road exit. Head northeast on Friant Road for 9.7 miles to the signed left turn into the Lost Lake Recreation Area. Follow the park road for 0.4 mile to the entrance station. Go left from the entrance station, and follow the park road for another 0.5 mile to a Y at the end of the developed area along the riverfront. Go right to the signed parking area for the nature trail. GPS: N36 58.279' / W119 44.316'

The Hike

Hikes on the urban interface often bring into sharp relief the value—and the challenges—of preserving parkland near cities. The Lost Lake Nature Trail, which explores a 70-acre nature-study area on the San Joaquin River, highlights this juxtaposition. Rambling along the overgrown banks of the San Joaquin River below the Friant Dam, the trail threads through an environment that provides habitat for eagles and is blessed by the calming, unceasing flow of the river . . . while graffiti on tree trunks and rock outcroppings is an unavoidable reminder of human disregard for that environment.

View the graffiti as art, and it is a little easier to merge nature with the tags. And the value of the trail—of the 305-acre Lost Lake Recreation Area as a whole—is undeniable. More developed areas of the park, with picnic facilities, campsites, and river access, are a popular escape for locals. The trail also offers river access, and with its thick riparian canopy, which includes red willow and Fremont cotton-wood, it is a cool option when the temperatures begin to climb.

The track's intimacy with the river is demonstrated in the trail surface, which varies from dirt singletrack and road to packed sand and river cobbles. When the water is high, the trail can be flooded (as it was when I explored it in the spring of 2011, a particularly wet season). Regardless of when you go, or how far you can go, the trail still offers escape and the chance to commune with the San Joaquin. Birders will be especially entranced, with songbirds flitting through the brush, waterfowl on the broad river, and eagles and hawks overhead.

The signed nature trail begins at the edge of the picnic area, and plunges almost immediately into the riparian zone. The river is on the west (right) as you head downstream, screened by thick willow and brush, and a steep embankment rises to the left. Lost Lake itself lies on the top of the embankment, comprised of former gravel pits that have filled with water.

Social paths weave from the main trail to the river. As you proceed, you'll pass the site of a fire pit ("tree art" is prevalent here). The trail narrows and grows a bit wilder beyond, snaking through the floodplain. The turnaround point is at 0.6 mile, where water prevented further progress, but you can continue downstream as far as conditions permit.

Lost Lake is the focus of a long-term improvement project, in the planning stages as of spring 2011, involving state and local government and private agencies (including the San Joaquin River Parkway and Conservation Trust). The goal is to improve all aspects of the park, from habitat restoration and trail construction to new and improved active recreational facilities such as boat launches. The park also encompasses a pair of native food-processing sites (bedrock mortars).

Miles and Directions

0.0 Start at the signed trailhead, passing a covered picnic site.

0.1 Pass a cluster of boulders marred by graffiti; a picnic shelter is visible atop the bluff. Stay left at all social trails leading right to the river.

0.3 The trail is intersected by a dirt track that comes in from the left (from atop the embankment). A fire pit, litter, and graffiti on the trees attest to the site's popularity. Continue on the

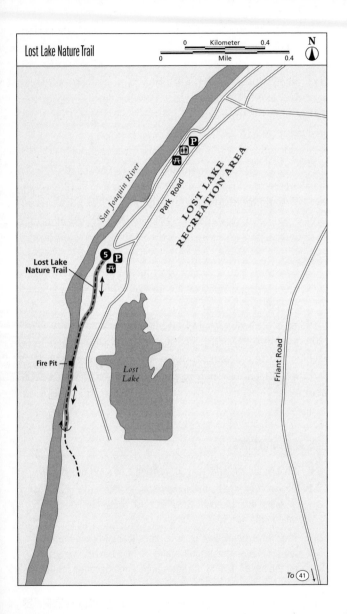

Lost Lake Nature Trail

0 Kilometer 0.4
0 Mile 0.4

N

San Joaquin River

P

LOST LAKE RECREATION AREA

Park Road

5 P

Lost Lake Nature Trail

Fire Pit

Lost Lake

Friant Road

To 41

obvious nature trail, which quickly resumes its more wildland nature.

0.6 Arrive at the turnaround point, with social trails leading to the riverfront. If conditions permit and you are willing, continue downstream. Otherwise, retrace your steps.

1.2 Arrive back at the trailhead.

6 South Shore Trail at Millerton Lake

Follow a flat, easy trail around McKenzie Point and out to Winchell Cove, enjoying views across Millerton Lake and up into the foothills as you hike.

Distance: 3.6 miles out and back

Approximate hiking time: 2 hours

Difficulty: Easy

Trail surface: Dirt singletrack

Best seasons: Late fall, winter, spring

Other trail users: Mountain bikers

Canine compatibility: Leashed dogs permitted

Fees and permits: An entry fee is charged.

Schedule: Open daily year-round from sunrise to sunset

Trailhead facilities: Paved parking area, restrooms, trashcans. Overflow parking is available back along the access road at the picnic area and at the boat launch.

Maps: USGS Friant CA and Millerton Lake West CA; online at www.parks.ca.gov (search for Millerton Lake SRA)

Trail contact: Millerton Lake State Recreation Area, 5290 Millerton Rd., Friant 93626; (559) 822-2332; www.parks.ca.gov

Finding the trailhead: From Fresno, follow CA 41 (the Yosemite Freeway) north. Take the Friant Road exit, and head northeast on Friant Road for about 11 miles to Millerton Road (at the junction with CR 206 below Friant Dam). Follow Millerton Road for 1.7 miles to the signed entrance to Millerton Lake State Recreation Area on the left. From the entry station, continue on the park road for about 2 miles to the parking area and trailhead at the road's end. GPS: N37 00.028' / W119 40.692'

The Hike

The site of a drowned gold rush town, submerged under more than 500,000 acre-feet of water (water enough to cover 500,000 acres to a depth of 1 foot), is now Fresno's best, closest choice for outdoor fun. Millerton Lake State Recreation Area, located on the Madera/Fresno county line at the base of the foothills, is easy to access, scenic, and friendly, making it popular with boaters, anglers, campers, and hikers.

Millerton, the lake's namesake, was once a thriving nineteenth-century burg, as evidenced by its designation as the Fresno county seat. But in 1867 the San Joaquin River overran its banks, the town was destroyed by the flood, and shortly thereafter the county seat moved to neighboring Fresno. The town launched into a decades-long decline, fading from argonaut mecca to quiet ranching community, with the imposing Millerton County Courthouse a reminder of its onetime prosperity.

When construction on the Friant Dam began in 1940, the Millerton town site was destined for submersion. The historic courthouse was dismantled and reassembled on a hilltop overlooking the 319-foot concrete dam and the sprawling lake behind it, a picturesque artifact from California's early days of statehood.

Millerton Lake is also home to the San Joaquin Valley's largest population of wintering bald eagles, and the South Shore (or Blue Oak) Trail offers some of the best vantage points from which to look for these majestic raptors. Golden eagles reside in the area year-round, as do a variety of other birds and mammals, from mountain lions to cottontail rabbits. While it's probably better not to encounter a mountain

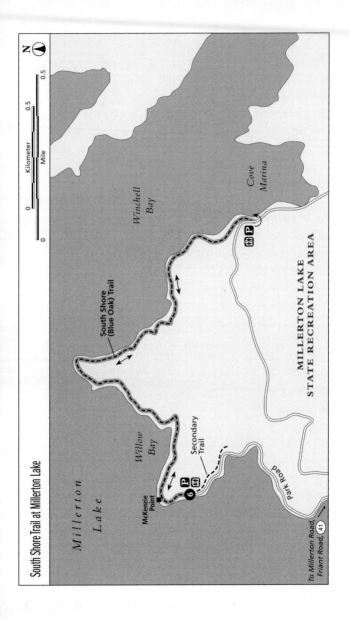

South Shore Trail at Millerton Lake

lion on the trail, it's a fairly sure bet that you'll see songbirds and ground squirrels as you hike.

The route begins at the end of the paved access road. The dam, courthouse, and lake form the views looking west. Vistas east to the Sierra divide (some overlook spots are outfitted with viewing benches) improve as you round McKenzie Point and begin the traverse toward Winchell Cove. A series of beaches, larger or smaller depending on the lake level, can be reached by branching left from the trail toward the lake, and scattered oaks offer shade, though on hot summer days these may be woefully inadequate. Activity on the lake, depending on the season, can range from perfectly quiet (in winter) to noisy and boisterous (when boaters crowd the lake in summer).

The trail leads, without interruption by intersections, to Winchell Cove, where boats are moored at floating docks. Look for raptors along the way, including migrating bald eagles, resident golden eagles, and hawks. Elegant blue herons and other shorebirds may also be present. The "white house," a striking structure with wraparound porches, overlooks the cove. The big paved parking lot (with restroom) at Winchell Cove is the turnaround point; from here, retrace your steps to the trailhead.

Miles and Directions

- **0.0** Begin by taking the signed singletrack trail alongside the restroom building.
- **0.3** Pass the second of several viewing benches and beach coves.
- **0.8** Round a bend, and the Winchell Cove boat dock comes into view. The shoreline is rockier, and large granite boulders dot the meadowlands above the trail.

1.1 A little docking hut floats in the cove below the trail, and a fenced utility station is on the right.

1.6 Pass a covered picnic site overlooking the Winchell Cove marina. A staircase leads down to the beach.

1.8 Negotiate an up-and-down stretch of trail, with rocky patches, before arriving at trail's end at the parking area for Winchell Cove. Return as you came.

3.6 Arrive back at the trailhead.

7 Buzzard's Roost at Millerton Lake

The climb to Buzzard's Roost will test your lungs and legs, but views from the summit are superlative and ample reward for the effort, stretching east across Millerton Lake into the San Joaquin Valley and west into the Sierra Nevada.

Distance: 1.2 miles out and back

Approximate hiking time: 1 hour

Difficulty: More challenging due to steepness

Trail surface: Dirt singletrack

Best seasons: Late fall, spring

Other trail users: None

Canine compatibility: Leashed dogs permitted

Fees and permits: A day-use fee is charged.

Schedule: Open daily year-round from sunrise to sunset

Trailhead facilities: None, but restrooms, water, camping, and picnic facilities are nearby.

Maps: USGS Millerton Lake West CA; online at www.parks.ca.gov (search for Millerton Lake SRA)

Special considerations: Given the trail's steepness and uneven surface, hikers with knee, heart, or lung problems should not attempt it.

Trail contact: Millerton Lake State Recreation Area, 5290 Millerton Rd., Friant 93626; (559) 822-2332; www.parks.ca.gov

Finding the trailhead: From Fresno, follow CA 41 (the Yosemite Freeway) north and east to its junction with CA 145 (Road 145, signed for the Millerton Lake SRA camping areas). Turn right on Road 145 and go 4.7 miles to the junction with Road 211. Turn right to stay on Road 145 (a sign points you to the Millerton Lake SRA) and drive into the park. The fee station is at 2.5 miles. The trailhead is 1.5 miles farther along the park road, on the left-hand side. There is parking for six or seven cars along the road on the right. The trailhead is well signed. GPS: N37 01.728' / W119 40.424'

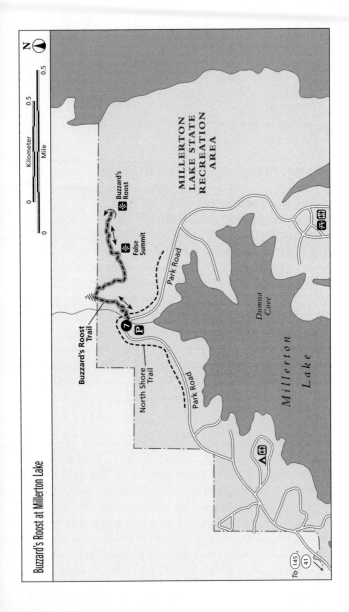

Buzzard's Roost at Millerton Lake

The Hike

This is a hiker's hike, straight up and straight down. The 500-foot elevation gain from trailhead to Buzzard's Roost is formidable, given the short distance. But that 0.6-mile one-way length is just what qualifies this route as easy—set a pace that's reasonable, rest when you need to, and you'll make it to the top with no trouble.

Your sweat and breathlessness will be well rewarded. From the roost (which you likely will, indeed, share with circling buzzards), you can see east across the foothills to the high peaks of the Sierra crest, and south and west across shimmering Millerton Lake to Friant Dam, the San Joaquin Valley, and, if the air is clear, the shadowy coast ranges. The boats and islands in the lake look tiny from the 1,058-foot perch, and the vistas are expansive.

The trail is straightforward, with obvious rest stops at the trickling waterfall fed by a seasonal stream that spills over a duff-colored rock face (a feature most impressive during the winter and spring), a break in a rangeland fence, a false summit, and the summit itself. The trail is well defined and broken with water bars and rocky stair steps, which help in the ascent. Once you reach the top, scramble through the lupine onto the rock outcrop and see what the buzzards see. When you've taken it all in, return as you came.

A few fun buzzard (aka turkey vulture) facts to contemplate as you climb . . . You can distinguish these scavengers from more "elegant" raptors in flight by their wobble: They tend to be tippy, dipping wingtips side to side as they glide. They also pee on their own feet and legs to keep cool on hot days. And vultures tend to vomit when stressed, such as when they are threatened by a predator. Scientists think the upchuck serves two purposes: to lighten the bird's load so it can escape quickly, and to leave a tasty (or foul) meal behind for the predator.

Miles and Directions

0.0 Begin by passing the trailhead signboard, with warnings about poison oak. The Buzzard's Roost and North Shore Trails meet at the sign; go left and uphill on the Buzzard's Roost Trail.

0.2 Pass the little waterfall (a use trail leads left to its summit). Stay right on the Buzzard's Roost Trail. About 200 feet beyond, pass a sign that reads 6-7.

0.3 Climb to lake views and a break in a rangeland fence. Pass the break and continue uphill.

0.4 Reach the false summit—a rock outcrop—and enjoy the views. Then continue up.

0.6 Pass through a saddle, then arrive at the Buzzard's Roost. Rest atop the rock outcrop, then retrace your steps to the trailhead.

1.2 Arrive back at the trailhead.

8 Bridge Trail (San Joaquin River Gorge)

Drop through oak woodland into the San Joaquin River Gorge, where a narrow suspension bridge spans the gray-walled river canyon.

Distance: 2.0 miles out and back
Approximate hiking time: 1.5 hours
Difficulty: Moderate due to elevation change
Trail surface: Dirt singletrack
Best seasons: Fall, winter, spring
Other trail users: Mountain bikers
Canine compatibility: Leashed dogs permitted
Fees and permits: None, though a day-use fee may be charged starting in 2012
Schedule: Open daily year-round
Trailhead facilities: Paved parking area, restrooms, picnic area, water, trashcans, information signboard. A visitor center, reconstructed native village, and camping facilities are also located in the recreation area.
Maps: USGS Millerton Lake East CA; map posted on signboard at trailhead; online at www.blm.gov/ca/st/en/fo/bakersfield/Programs/Recreation_opportunities/sjrg_map.html
Trail contact: San Joaquin River Gorge Special Recreation Management Area, Bureau of Land Management Bakersfield Field Office, 3801 Pegasus Dr., Bakersfield 93308; (661) 391-6000; www.blm.gov/ca/st/en/fo/bakersfield/Programs/Recreation_opportunities/SJRG_SRMA.htm. Visitor center: (559) 855-3492

Finding the trailhead: From Fresno and Clovis, pick up CA 168 and head east toward the foothills town of Auberry. Pass through Prather, then turn left onto Auberry Road. Follow Auberry Road for

2.9 miles to Powerhouse Road (Power House Number 1 Road). Turn left on Powerhouse Road and go 1.9 mile to Smalley Road (with a sign for the San Joaquin River Gorge). Turn left on Smalley Road and continue 4.3 miles to the recreation area near the river. At the sign stay left (downhill) for 0.1 mile to the Ya-Gub-Weh-Tuh trailhead on the right. GPS: N37 04.973' / W119 33.249'

The Hike

The San Joaquin River gets a squeeze in the gray-walled canyon at the turnaround point of this scenic trail. Funneled through narrows downstream from the picturesque Kerckhoff Powerhouse, the river in the gorge is spanned by a slender suspension bridge that allows you to stand high above and watch the water tumble from pool to pool below.

The hike down to the bridge and gorge is straightforward. It begins at the signed trailhead and drops through a pretty oak woodland directly toward the gorge. As you descend, breaks in the canopy allow glimpses of the brick-colored rimrock high atop the canyon wall and east up the narrowing river valley. Wildflowers bloom in profusion in March and April, with orange fiddlenecks among the first to emerge, distinctive with their fern-frondlike curls.

As you begin a declining traverse, power lines become visible, a reminder of how the San Joaquin has been harnessed by a series of dams (including the Friant Dam not far downstream and the Kerckhoff Dam not far upstream) to provide hydroelectric power and fill irrigation canals for Central Valley farms below. The terrain is drier on this slope, with scrub oak and foothills chaparral bordering the path.

The trail leads past a gate and spur trail, with the rocky canyon walls now clearly visible below. Negotiate a couple

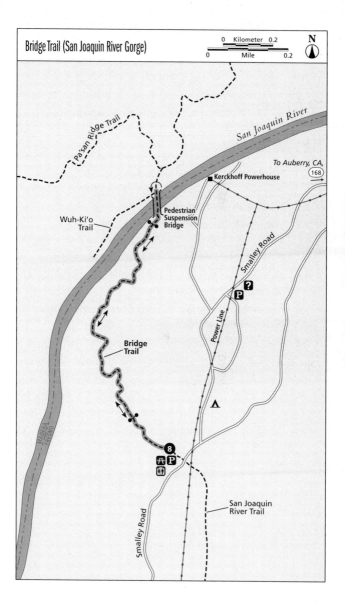

Bridge Trail (San Joaquin River Gorge)

0   Kilometer   0.2
0   Mile   0.2

N

Pa'san Ridge Trail

San Joaquin River

To Auberry, CA, 168

Kerckhoff Powerhouse

Wuh-Ki'o Trail

Pedestrian Suspension Bridge

Smalley Road

Power Line

Bridge Trail

MADERA
FRESNO

8

San Joaquin River Trail

Smalley Road

of easy switchbacks and the bridge, with its pale green arches and slender pedestrian walkway, comes into view. A final short set of stairs brings you to the bridge's near-shore anchor. Snap your pictures, walk across the bridge and back, gawking at the swirl of the San Joaquin below, then retrace your steps to the trailhead. It's all uphill from here.

Miles and Directions

0.0 Start by descending past the trailhead sign on the single-track trail.

0.1 Pass a gate.

0.3 Skirt a gully, then views of the gorge open.

0.6 Power lines become visible. Cross a seasonal stream that flows into spring and dries as the summer progresses.

0.8 Pass a second gate. A spur trail departs to the right; stay left on the obvious main path.

1.0 A set of steps leads to the bridge. Cross the span, then head back the way you came.

2.0 Arrive back at the trailhead.

Options: Two trail extensions lie on the far side of the bridge. The Pa'san Ridge Trail, popular with mountain bikers, forms a 6.0-mile loop; total mileage for this route is 8.0 miles. The Wuh-ki'o Trail runs 2.5 miles out-and-back down the San Joaquin River, for a 7.0-mile round-trip trek.

9 San Joaquin River Trail

Traverse through oak woodlands on the lower slopes of Squaw Leap before dropping to a hidden water course and a spectacular bridge at the confluence of Big Sandy Creek and the San Joaquin River.

Distance: 5.1 miles out and back

Approximate hiking time: 3 hours

Difficulty: More challenging due to length and elevation change

Trail surface: Dirt singletrack

Best seasons: Fall, winter, spring

Other trail users: Mountain bikers

Canine compatibility: Leashed dogs permitted

Fees and permits: None, though a day-use fee may be charged starting in 2012

Schedule: Open daily year-round

Trailhead facilities: Paved parking area, restrooms, picnic area, water, trashcans, information signboard. A visitor center, reconstructed native village, and camping facilities are also in the recreation area.

Maps: USGS Millerton Lake East CA; map posted on the signboard at trailhead; online at www.blm.gov/ca/st/en/fo/bakersfield/Programs/Recreation_opportunities/sjrg_map.html

Trail contact: San Joaquin River Gorge Special Recreation Management Area, Bureau of Land Management Bakersfield Field Office, 3801 Pegasus Dr., Bakersfield 93308; (661) 391-6000; www.blm.gov/ca/st/en/fo/bakersfield/Programs/Recreation_opportunities/SJRG_SRMA.htm. Visitor center: (559) 855-3492

Finding the trailhead: From Fresno and Clovis, take CA 168 east toward the foothills town of Auberry. Pass through Prather, then turn left off CA 168 onto Auberry Road. Follow Auberry Road for 2.9 miles to Powerhouse Road (Power House Number 1 Road). Turn left on

Powerhouse Road and go 1.9 miles to Smalley Road (with a sign for the San Joaquin River Gorge). Turn left on Smalley Road and continue 4.3 miles to the recreation area near the river. At the sign stay left (downhill) for 0.1 mile to the Ya-Gub-Weh-Tuh trailhead on the right. Park here, then cross the road to the signed trailhead. GPS: N37 04.954' / W119 33.230'

The Hike

Impossible, spectacular bridges seem to be a common theme in the San Joaquin River Gorge. Down at the rocky confluence with Big Sandy Creek, a modern span, airlifted into place by helicopter, marks the turnaround point for this route.

The bridge is just one segment in an ambitious, long-term plan to extend the San Joaquin River Trail from Fresno to the Devils Postpile National Monument near the eastern slope of the Sierra Nevada. Spearheaded by the San Joaquin River Trail Council, a diverse consortium of trail advocates that includes the Sierra Club, Central California Off-Road Cyclists, and the Back Country Horsemen of California, plans call for the route to link historic and existing trails for more than 77 miles. Some of the trail segments trace Mono Indian trade routes and routes used by gold miners.

This out-and-back trek is part of a longer, 14-mile stretch of trail that continues to Temperance Flat and into Millerton Lake State Recreation Area. It begins by rolling through oak woodlands at the base of Squaw Leap, the distinctive rimrock-capped peak on the east side of the river that rises to more than 2,300 feet. You'll hardly know you are descending for the first 2 miles or so, as you traverse the mountainside and enjoy views of the wooded hills to the west. Pass through a series of gullies as you proceed; carved by seasonal streams, the washes may be dry depending on the time of year.

While a number of native critters abide in the woodland, including deer, squirrels, and a variety of birds, cows also roam the landscape. Gentle, skittish creatures, they will likely scatter as you approach, or mark your passage with big, mild eyes. Be sure to close all gates behind you.

Another unnatural feature is the power line, which drops from the Kerckhoff Powerhouse upstream. On the upland part of the hike, the lines and towers are constant companions, but in the river bottom they are out of sight and out of mind.

The trail presents a more vigorous descent just beyond the 1.5-mile mark, with the rocky riverbed flicking in and out of view. Pass a pair of gates at the end of the steep descent, and begin a gentle traverse along the riverside with unimpeded views of the waterway. You'll have to climb to get back to the trailhead, but set a steady pace and it'll be no problem.

Finish the trek at riverside, hiking first to a jumble of rocks that hides a water course. It's noisy enough in early season to mimic a waterfall, flows unseen under the trail, and issues into the river downstream at a sandbar (depending on the water level). The bridge on Big Sandy Creek and the turnaround point are just downstream. Retrace your steps to the trailhead.

Miles and Directions

0.0 Begin at the signed trailhead across the road from the parking area. The packed singletrack trail leads through a gate less than 0.1 mile from the trailhead.

0.1 Pass under the power line.

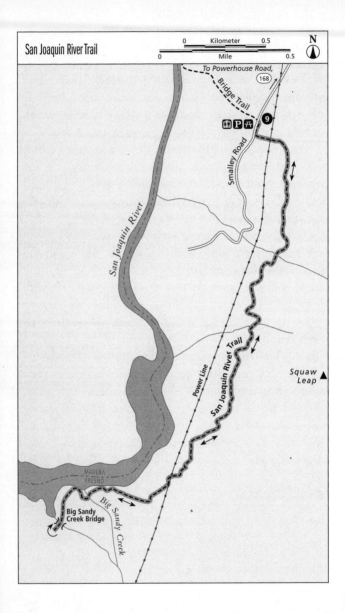

0.3 Roll through the first of several gullies. These are spaced approximately 0.1 mile distant from one another.

0.6 Roll through the fourth gully, distinguished by a growth of willow and followed by a stand of spindly digger pines.

0.9 Pass a battered trail post. A large water tank is to the right.

1.3 Hike through another streamlet and stand of pines.

1.6 Traverse through some pines then negotiate a brief, steep, downhill pitch. The trail descends from here on out, sometimes steeply.

2.1 Pass a gate with a stile and enjoy the river views.

2.25 Pass a second gate. The trail runs riverside.

2.4 Arrive at the rock jumble that hides a side stream.

2.5 Reach the Big Sandy Creek Bridge and the turnaround point. Retrace your steps from here.

5.1 Arrive back at the trailhead.

10 Buck Ridge Loop at Hensley Lake

Follow rolling trails and dirt roads into the sparse oak woodlands on the east shore of Hensley Lake. The return leg of the loop offers access to the shoreline and flat rocks for picnicking and sunbathing.

Distance: 3.1-mile lollipop
Approximate hiking time: 1.5 hours
Difficulty: Easy
Trail surface: Dirt singletrack and dirt roadway
Best seasons: Fall, winter, spring
Other trail users: Mountain bikers, equestrians
Canine compatibility: Leashed dogs permitted
Fees and permits: A day-use fee is charged.
Schedule: Open daily year-round from sunrise to sunset
Trailhead facilities: Paved parking area, restrooms, trashcans, disc golf course, information signboard. Additional restrooms, a boat launch, picnic facilities, and a tot lot lie farther down the Buck Ridge Day-Use Area access road.

Maps: USGS Little Table Mountain CA and Daulton CA; online at www.spk.usace.army.mil/organizations/cespk-co/lakes/buck_ridge_trail.pdf; available from the park office located on the southwest side of the lake
Other: Campsites are available at the Hidden View Campground. The visitor center, open Mon through Fri from 7:45 a.m. to 4:30 p.m., is located in the park headquarters. Follow signs off Road 603 to reach the center.
Trail contact: US Army Corps of Engineers Hensley Lake, P.O. Box 85, Raymond 93653-0085; (559) 673-5151; www.spk.usace.army.mil/organizations/cespk-co/lakes/hensley.html

Finding the trailhead: From Fresno, head north on CA 41 to CA 145. Turn left (west) on CA 145 and drive about 8.5 miles to the junction with Road 33. Turn right (north) on Road 33 and go about 1 mile to the intersection with Road 400 (River Road). Go right (northeast) on Road 400 for about 8.8 miles to the signed turnoff for the Buck Ridge Day-Use Area (on the left/west).

Alternatively, take CA 99 north to Madera. Take the exit for CA 145 (Yosemite Avenue) and follow CA 145 about 4 miles east to its junction with Road 400/River Road. Follow Road 400 for about 12.5 miles to the turn for Buck Ridge. The turnoff is about 1.7 miles beyond the sign for Hensley Lake at the junction with Road 603/Daulton Road.

Pay the day-use fee, then follow the park road about 0.1 mile to the trailhead parking area on the right. GPS: N37 07.287' / W119 52.144'

The Hike

Views of the rolling, oak-studded landscape surrounding Hensley Lake are abundant from the Buck Ridge trail system, which meanders along roadways and pathways on the lake's east shore. From high points along the route (and there are a few, involving short bits of stiff climbing), you can also look west into the foothills of the Sierra Nevada. Where the views end the relaxation begins: A number of granite slabs can be found on the section of trail that runs along the lake's shoreline, inviting hikers to drop their packs, lay back on the warm rock, and soak up some rays.

Hensley Lake is hemmed in behind Hidden Dam, built between 1972 and 1975 to impound the flow of the Fresno River. The reservoir provides for flood control and irrigation, as well as supports a thriving recreation area. In addition to hiking, visitors to Hensley Lake enjoy great fishing in the coves, hooking black bass, bluegill, catfish, and other game fish, as well as rainbow trout that are stocked in winter. Two boat ramps allow water-skiers, sailors, and other boaters access to the lake. Equestrians and mountain bikers share the trails in the Buck Ridge area as well.

The Buck Ridge Trail consists of interlocking color-coded paths and access roads, with more than 8 miles of trail available. This route follows portions of the blue and green trails. Trail posts along the way feature colored arrows that help with route finding. There are a number of options, particularly for the green trail, so if you have the time and inclination, you can add to your explorations.

Begin by heading along a dirt roadway that leads north into the oak woodland. In winter and spring, when the water is high, ponds dot the landscape, including a rather large one fed by a vigorous stream to the right (east) of the trail. Just beyond this pond you'll encounter the first of a few rather steep climbs, as the trail negotiates folds in the hilly landscape. Views of the lake open to your left as you climb; to the right a rocky gully cradles the stream that feeds the pond. Once on top you'll enjoy great views across Hensley Lake.

Beyond the first high point, the trail roller-coasters through gullies and over hilltops before intersecting the green trail. The trail map shows a series of "green options" in this area; this route follows one of the best traveled paths, dropping back to the blue trail for the return leg along the shoreline.

The dirt, singletrack blue trail leads around coves and over grassy shoulders, offering wide-open lake views as it heads back toward the trailhead. Flat rocks begin to crop up just beyond the 2.0-mile mark, offering respite at points along the final portion of the loop.

When the blue trails converge on the dirt road, retrace your steps to the trailhead.

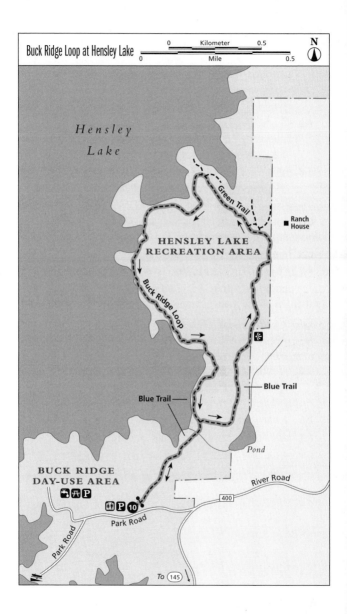

Buck Ridge Loop at Hensley Lake

0   Kilometer   0.5
0   Mile   0.5

N

Hensley Lake

Green Trail

■ Ranch House

HENSLEY LAKE RECREATION AREA

Buck Ridge Loop

Blue Trail

Blue Trail

Pond

BUCK RIDGE DAY-USE AREA

River Road

400

Park Road

Park Road

To 145

Miles and Directions

0.0 Start by passing the gate, a disc golf course hole, and hitching posts, following a dirt road marked with a trail post with blue and white arrows. The trail splits in less than 0.1 mile; stay left.

0.2 The blue trail splits. Stay right on the broad track. Use trails intersect the main route as you continue; stay on the obvious dirt roadway, sticking with the blue trail markers.

0.4 After crossing a stream drainage (requires log hopping in the rainy season) the trail splits. Follow the blue-arrow trail to the right.

0.5 Pass the fenced-off pond on the right. The trail begins its first short, steep climb.

0.8 Arrive atop a high point with commanding lake views.

1.1 Reach the junction with the green trail, marked with a trail post. The fence to the right delineates private property. Go left on the green trail, now a singletrack heading west toward the lake.

1.2 Green trails converge at the trail post. Stay left, heading toward the lakeshore.

1.5 At the next trail junction, go left on the blue trail. Two green-marked paths head to the right. The blue trail follows the shoreline, heading back toward the trailhead.

2.0 A trail joins from the left; stay straight on the main track.

2.1 Another use trail joins from the left; stay straight.

2.4 Pass another trail on the left but continue straight ahead. Reach rock outcrops that make for perfect sunning and picnicking platforms.

2.5 Pass yet another trail coming in from the left. Stay straight, hiking down a rocky gully.

2.7 Close the blue loop by meeting up with the dirt road that leads back to the trailhead. Retrace your steps.

3.1 Arrive back at the trailhead.

11 Monument Ridge at Eastman Lake

The rolling hills and rocky shorelines bordering Eastman Lake are showcased on these two easy out-and-back trails. The first leg follows the waterline, while the second leads back into more secluded country.

Distance: 3.7 miles total for 2 out-and-back trails; first trail is 1.5 miles out and back; the second is 2.2 miles out and back

Approximate hiking time: 2 hours

Difficulty: Easy

Trail surface: Dirt singletrack (waterfront trail); dirt access road (Wildlife Management Area trail)

Best seasons: Fall, winter, spring

Other trail users: Mountain bikers, equestrians

Canine compatibility: Leashed dogs permitted

Fees and permits: A day-use fee is charged.

Schedule: Open daily year-round

Trailhead facilities: Large paved parking area, trashcans, information signboard. Restrooms and picnic facilities are a few hundred feet back down the access road at the disc golf course.

Maps: USGS Raymond CA; map in brochure available at the trailhead

Special considerations: Hunting is permitted in the Wildlife Management Area (and on the Lakeview Trail). Be aware of your fellow trail users and wear bright colors.

Trail contact: US Army Corp of Engineers, Eastman Lake, P.O. Box 67, Raymond 93653-0067; (559) 689-3255; corpslakes.us ace.army.mil/visitors/projects .cfm?Id=L268004; www.spk .usace.army.mil/organizations/ cespk-co/lakes/eastman.html

Finding the trailhead: From Fresno, follow CA 99 north to Chowchilla. Take exit 233, signed for Raymond and Eastman Lake. Go east on Avenue 26 for 12.9 miles to Road 29. Go left on Road 29

for 8.5 miles, past the fee station, to the signed road for the Monument Day-Use Area at the base of Buchanan Dam.

Alternatively, you can take CA 99 north to Madera. Take the Cleveland Avenue exit. Take Road 26 north to Avenue 26. Follow Avenue 26 east to Road 29. Go left on Road 29 for 8.5 miles into the recreation area.

Follow the park road for 1.0 mile to a signed left turn onto the access road for the Monument Ridge trailhead. Continue for 0.4 mile to the road's end, passing the disc golf course, restrooms, and picnic area to the trailhead parking lot. GPS: N37 13.968' / W119 59.158'

The Hike

Eastman Lake, one of several Army Corps of Engineers facilities in the San Joaquin Valley, performs multiple functions for residents and visitors to the Fresno area. Recreation is the most pertinent with regard to hikers, but in addition to hosting several trails, the lake and its surroundings are also used by boaters, campers, anglers, and hunters. The water stored behind Buchanan Dam, which bottles up the Chowchilla River, is used for irrigation, and the dam helps control flooding on the river.

The lake's surroundings are quintessentially Californian, with sprawling oaks dotting meadowlands thick with wildflowers in spring. The nonnative grasses, imported from Spain on the hooves of cattle in the days of the missionaries, green up beautifully with winter rains, and dry to a brittle gold during the long, hot summer. The oaks are sparse on the hillsides, offering only a little shade, and gray granite rock outcrops stand out against the golds and greens of the flora, especially on the east side of the lake.

There are several focal points for outdoorspeople on the lake. The Codorniz area, with campgrounds, a boat ramp, an equestrian area, and access to the Lakeview Trail (8.0 miles out and back to the Raymond Bridge), lies along the southeast edge of the lake. The Monument Ridge and Chowchilla recreation areas are on the west shore of the lake and also feature a boat ramp, hiking, hunters' access, and a disc golf course.

The two out-and-back trails described here are on Monument Ridge. The first trail heads downhill from the trailhead to the lakeside, offering views up into the Sierran highlands. The path then skirts the shoreline (water levels vary depending on runoff and releases) south to the Chowchilla boat ramp. Traveling through a sparse oak woodland, the singletrack path features wonderful lake views and access to fishing coves.

The second trail heads north from the parking area and follows a dirt access road into the Wildlife Management Area. Near the trail's outset you'll pass an old windmill and a fenced-off water tank; the windmill sounds squeaky and sad as it turns, a haunting sound. Beyond, the trail roller-coasters gently uphill through open oak woodland, offering views of both the lake and the Sierra foothills through breaks in the grass-covered hills. Watch for eagles and hawks circling overhead and alighting on the skeletal branches of deciduous oaks in winter and spring. Spring brings an amazing wildflower bloom.

After climbing for a bit, the trail drops down to near the lakeshore (depending on lake level). Islands dot the water, bigger or smaller (again, depending on lake level). The access road continues around the shoreline. Turn around where the trail bears west; the grasslands or rocky outcrops offer great picnic and rest stops. Retrace your steps to the trailhead.

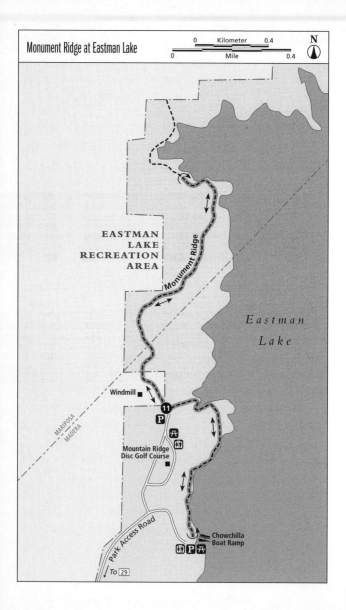

Monument Ridge at Eastman Lake

N

0   Kilometer   0.4

0   Mile   0.4

EASTMAN
LAKE
RECREATION
AREA

Monument Ridge

Eastman
Lake

Windmill

11
P

Mountain Ridge
Disc Golf Course

MARIPOSA

MADERA

Chowchilla
Boat Ramp

Park Access Road

To 29

Miles and Directions

0.0 Start at the signed trail on the east side of the parking area, descending on singletrack toward the lake.

0.1 Arrive at a little cove and bear right on the trail.

0.4 Roll southward through open grassland to views of the lake and dam.

0.6 A riparian thicket crowds the trail as it passes a seasonal streamlet and a nice rock outcropping.

0.75 Drop through a shady drainage and then reach the Chowchilla boat ramp parking area, with restrooms and water. Retrace your steps to Monument Ridge.

1.5 Back at Monument Ridge, pass the gate onto the Wildlife Management Area access road.

1.6 Pass the windmill and water tank.

1.8 Head down and around the base of a hill topped with a distinctive window rock on the summit.

2.4 A steep pitch leads to the quiet lake backwaters.

2.6 Reach a stretch of trail overlooking a quiet cove. The hillside below the trail is grassy and offers great lake views, perfect for a picnic. A ranch house sits on the hill to the north. This is the turnaround point; retrace your route.

3.7 Arrive back at the trailhead.

12 Way-of-the-Mono Trail at Bass Lake

Interpretive signs along this forested trail overlooking scenic Bass Lake describe how indigenous peoples who once lived in the foothills east of Fresno used their environmental resources.

Distance: 1.1-mile loop
Approximate hiking time: 1 hour
Difficulty: Easy
Trail surface: Dirt singletrack, forest road
Best seasons: Late spring, summer, fall
Other trail users: None
Canine compatibility: Leashed dogs permitted
Fees and permits: None
Schedule: Open daily year-round from sunrise to sunset

Trailhead facilities: Small paved parking area, information sign. Restrooms and more parking are available across Road 222 at the Little Denver Church Picnic Area.
Maps: USGS Bass Lake CA; available at the Bass Lake Ranger Station on Road 222
Trail contact: Bass Lake Ranger District (Sierra National Forest), 57003 Road 225, North Fork 93643; (559) 877-2218; www .fs.fed.us/r5/sierra

Finding the trailhead: From Fresno, head north and east on CA 41 toward Oakhurst. About 3 miles beyond Oakhurst, turn right off CA 41 onto Road 222, signed for Bass Lake. Follow Road 222 for 3.3 miles to its junction with Road 274; bear right on Road 222 (Saddleback). Bear right again 0.3 mile farther, staying on Road 222. Continue on Road 222 for 1.5 miles, passing the ranger station, to the signed Way-of-the-Mono trailhead on the right. GPS: N37 19.306' / W119 34.677'

The Hike

The Mono Indians were among the indigenous inhabitants of the Sierra Nevada's western slope. A hunting and gathering society, the Mono ranged along the mountain front between Yosemite and Lake Kaweah before the arrival of Spanish colonists in the late 1700s, migrating with the seasons, the availability of game, and the ripening of staple food sources (such as acorns). Like many California Indian tribes, they lived in harmony with their environment and used what nature provided to build shelters, create trade goods, and support their spiritual belief systems.

Aspects of how the Mono used the forest surrounding what is now Bass Lake are described on interpretive signs along the Way-of-the-Mono Trail. The guide is Eku'Mina, a fictional ten-year-old Mono girl, the perfect companion for a hike that is perfect for modern children.

The trail begins by climbing into the fragrant woods, passing signs that describe how incense cedar bark was used to build homes and how the nuts of the black and live oak were used as food. The slope is fairly steep, with the path switchbacking alongside a drainage. It tops out on a large shelf of granite overlooking Bass Lake, which in the time of the Mono was a meadow. It wasn't until after the first dam was built in what became known as the Crane Valley that the lake formed.

The granite slabs are the perfect place to rest and explore. Look carefully for perfectly round holes in the rock, which are mortars once used by the Mono women to grind acorns into flour and meal.

The arrival of Europeans—members of the Mariposa Battalion, gold seekers, loggers, ranchers—meant the demise of the Mono way of life. Though some members of the tribe survived the old-world diseases that annihilated other California tribes, the inexorable forces of Manifest Destiny ultimately resulted in the loss of their land and livelihood.

The attractive valley that the Mono inhabited has been transformed into a lively recreation area. According to forest service literature, the first earthen dam in the valley was built by the San Joaquin Electric Company in 1901. This was later replaced by the more substantial structure that stands today, and campgrounds, boat launches, and other amenities were built around the reservoir. The lake and dam continue to provide electricity, as well as supply irrigation water to the San Joaquin Valley below.

You can return to the trailhead directly from the rock outcrop, but this route extends the forest exploration by climbing farther into the woods. Thick stands of manzanita, forming a bower over the trail in some spots, as well as mixed pines and cedars, envelope the path as you circle on unsigned but easy-to-follow forest roads and trails to meet up with the Way-of-the-Mono Trail at the base of the outcrop. You'll cross the creek as it issues from a rock jumble below the outcrop and tumbles down slabs toward the lake. From the creek, drop through more woods to the trailhead.

Miles and Directions

0.0 Start by passing the information sign and heading uphill on the narrow woodland trail, passing the first interpretive sign.

0.1 Switchbacks aid the climb alongside the drainage. Pass the sign about poison oak.

0.25 Arrive at the top of the rock outcrop. After resting, exploring, and checking out the views, pick up the trail that climbs up

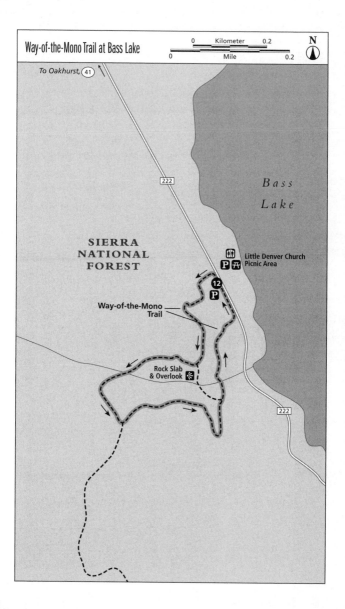

Way-of-the-Mono Trail at Bass Lake

0 Kilometer 0.2

0 Mile 0.2

N

To Oakhurst, 41

222

Bass Lake

SIERRA NATIONAL FOREST

Little Denver Church Picnic Area

12

Way-of-the-Mono Trail

Rock Slab & Overlook

222

the left (north) side of the outcrop. Pass a bench and then ascend through thick stands of manzanita.

0.5 Cross a rock slab and ford a creek (rock- and log-hopping if the water is high).

0.6 Meet the old forest road. Go left for less than 0.1 mile to an unsigned but obvious road/trail that drops downhill to the left. Take this wide trail downhill.

0.8 The trail narrows and becomes rutted before reaching a clearing. In the clearing, take the unsigned path that heads sharply left.

0.9 Meet the Way-of-the-Mono track, with the base of the rock outcrop to the left. Drop down a switchback and around the base of the rock, crossing the creek.

1.1 Arrive back at the trailhead.

Options: Several other trails around Bass Lake offer more-challenging hiking options. The Goat Mountain and Spring Cove Trails, on the south side of Bass Lake, lead several miles to the Goat Mountain lookout. The Willow Creek Trail, on the north side of the lake, leads to Angel Falls and Devils Slide.

13 Lewis Creek National Scenic Trail

A series of cascades and waterfalls enliven this easy track, which climbs gently through the dense evergreen woodlands of the Sierra foothills.

Distance: 3.6 miles out and back

Approximate hiking time: 2.5 hours

Difficulty: Moderate due to trail length

Trail surface: Dirt singletrack

Best seasons: Spring, summer, fall

Other trail users: Mountain bikers, equestrians

Canine compatibility: Leashed dogs permitted

Fees and permits: None

Schedule: Open daily year-round

Trailhead facilities: Paved parking lot

Maps: USGS Fish Camp CA; National Geographic Trails Illustrated Shaver Lake map; online at www.fs.fed.us/r5/sierra/pub lications/maps/fish-camp.htm (forest map; click on Fish Camp quadrant)

Trail contact: Sierra National Forest, 1600 Tollhouse Rd., Clovis 93611; (559) 297-0706; www.fs.fed.us/r5/sierra

Finding the trailhead: From Fresno, follow CA 41 northeast to the foothills town of Oakhurst. Continue northeast from Oakhurst on CA 41 for about 7 miles to the paved roadside parking area and trailhead on the right, just beyond the 4,000-foot-elevation sign. The trailhead is at the east end of the lot, marked by a gate and a sign that reads 21E06. GPS: N37 24.988' / W119 37.568'

The Hike

Two forces of nature will strike you as you hike along the Lewis Creek drainage. The first is subtle: the smell. The

mixed conifer forest that thrives along the creek is power-
fully fragrant, with the scent of pine and incense cedar ema-
nating from the needles you crush under your feet as you
hike and from the bark of the trees themselves. The second
is more obvious: the creek. The waterway is vigorous and
noisy, tumbling in a series of falls and cascades visible and
visitable from the trail.

The easy pitch of the route between this trailhead
(located at about the middle of the trail's length) and the
turnaround point at Red Rock Falls can be attributed to
its forerunner—a 54-mile-long flume. Built and operated
by the Madera-Sugar Pine Lumber Company beginning
in 1900, the flume was used for more than thirty years to
transport a billion board feet of high-country timber to the
company's flatland mill. The incline was gentle enough that
the "herder," who walked a narrow catwalk alongside the
flume, could ensure the wood kept moving downhill.

Corlieu Falls, just downstream from the trailhead, is
named for Charles Corlieu, an outdoorsman who settled
near Shaver Lake in the late 1800s, making a living as a log-
ger and operator of a way station for travelers. According to
forest service literature, he became enamored of the Lewis
Creek area after visiting his daughter, who lived in the area.
He built a cabin overlooking the falls and vacationed at
the site, which was developed as a resort in the 1930s. All
signs of development have long since been removed, leaving the area as natural and magical as when Corlieu fell in
love with it.

The trail, part of the National Recreation Trails System,
is straightforward and obvious. After dropping into the
creek bottom, a split-log bridge deposits you on the east
side of the waterway and begins a slow, rolling climb up its

course. You'll have a number of opportunities to leave the path and follow spur trails to the creek side, where you can dip your feet if the flow is low enough and the day is hot enough. When the water is high, during winter and spring runoff, the thrill is getting close to the whitewater produced in the cascades. Beware of slippery rocks, but in general the granite boulders that hem in sections of the creek offer safe observation perches.

The trail is almost directly below CA 41, so road noise is fairly constant. Don't let this put you off. At times, especially when the water is high, the highway noise is drowned out by the sound of the creek. Little bridges span side streams at points along the route, ensuring that you won't have to get your feet wet unless you want to.

The turnaround point is at Red Rock Falls, though the trail climbs a short distance beyond to the Sugar Pine trailhead. Again, a spur trail (rather steep but well worn) leads down to overlook rocks atop the falls. The rocks are perfect for sunning; the water pools above the 10-foot falls and a cavelike alcove makes for an enticing picnic spot. Enjoy the joyful noise, then retrace your steps to the trailhead.

Miles and Directions

0.0 Start at the signed trailhead, dropping down the broad track past the gate.

0.1 At the trail T (with a sign), go left. The right fork leads downstream along Lewis Creek to Corlieu Falls and the Cedar Valley trailhead.

0.2 Cross the split-log bridge. On the other side of the creek, go left (upstream).

0.4 Cross a second split-log footbridge that spans a side stream. Just beyond, pass a huge boulder and a fire ring.

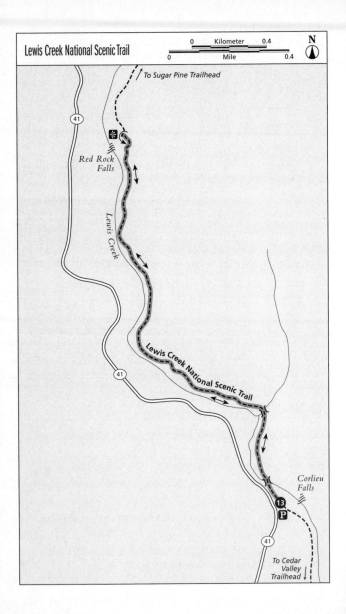

Lewis Creek National Scenic Trail

0   Kilometer   0.4
0   Mile   0.4

N

To Sugar Pine Trailhead

41

Red Rock
Falls

Lewis Creek

41

Lewis Creek National Scenic Trail

Corlieu
Falls

13
P

41

To Cedar
Valley
Trailhead

0.5 Pass a cascade.

0.7 At the next cascade, climb two switchbacks, staying to the right above the short spill. A spur trail leads left down to an overlook rock.

0.8 Cross a little bridge, then pass a stone foundation (one of Corlieu's cabins, perhaps?).

1.2 Cross another small bridge.

1.6 Cross yet another bridgelet; you can hear more than see Red Rock Falls, which are just ahead.

1.7 At a log staircase a side trail leads left down to the falls overlook.

1.8 Reach the top of the falls. Return the way you came.

3.6 Arrive back at the trailhead.

Option: If you'd like to lengthen your exploration of Lewis Creek trail, head downstream to Corlieu Falls and to the trail's end in Cedar Valley. Total round-trip distance for the entire route is about 7.4 miles.

14 North Fork Trail Tour

A pair of trails in the little town of North Fork offers glimpses into both the nature of the foothills and the ways in which humans have harnessed and utilized the region's resources.

Distance: 2.0 miles for two out-and-back trail legs. Manzanita Lake Flume is 0.8 mile out and back; the Cedars Interpretive Trail is 1.2 miles out and back.

Approximate hiking time: 30 to 45 minutes for the Manzanita Lake Flume; 1 hour for the Cedars Interpretive Trail

Difficulty: Easy

Trail surface: Old roadway and pavement for the Manzanita Lake Flume; dirt singletrack with paved patches and boardwalk for the Cedars Interpretive Trail

Best seasons: Spring, summer, fall

Other trail users: Mountain bikers and anglers on the Manzanita Lake Flume path; none on the Cedars Interpretive Trail

Canine compatibility: Leashed dogs permitted

Fees and permits: None

Schedule: Open daily year-round from sunrise to sunset

Trailhead facilities: Both trailheads have parking areas, restrooms, and picnic facilities. Bass Lake Ranger Station at the Cedars Interpretive Trail offers information.

Maps: USGS North Fork CA

Trail contact: Bass Lake Ranger District (Sierra National Forest), 57003 Road 225, North Fork 93643; (559) 877-2218; www .fs.fed.us/r5/sierra

Finding the trailhead: From Fresno, head north and east on CA 41 toward Oakhurst. About 3 miles above Oakhurst, turn right off CA 41 onto Road 222, signed for Bass Lake. Follow Road 222 for 3.3 miles to its junction with Road 274 at Bass Lake. Stay left on Road 274, which becomes Malum Ridge Road, for about 10.8 miles to its junction with Road 225/Minarets Road. Turn right onto Road 225

and go 0.3 mile to the Road 222 / Manzanita Road. Follow Manzanita Road for 1.7 miles to the Manzanita Lake Picnic Area. The trail
begins at the south end of the picnic area parking area. GPS for the
Manzanita Lake Flume: N37 14.834' / W119 31.106'

The Cedars Interpretive Trail is located at the Bass Lake Ranger
Station, off the signed access road just before the Manzanita Road
turnoff. Follow the access road for 0.3 mile to the ranger station
parking area and trailhead. GPS for Cedars Interpretive Trail: N37
13.947' / W119 30.537'

The Hike

These two short trails are located in the quaint little town
of North Fork, the "Exact Center of California." The first
path explores the shoreline, dam, and flume at little Manzanita Lake; the second explores the riparian habitat along
the north fork of Willow Creek.

The flume trail departs from the Manzanita Lake Picnic
Area and follows an old roadway along the wooded shoreline of the small lake. The trail deposits you at the junction
of paved service roads at the lake's dam, a wall of concrete
with a spillway that dumps overflow down a rock outcrop
and into a narrow gorge on Willow Creek. To reach the
flume, stay on the low road, walking a short distance to
where water issues from a tunnel and into the concrete
channel. Though a narrow metal walkway runs down
planks that span the top of the flume, this is the turnaround
point. Continuing down the flume is a hazardous (and far
from easy) proposition.

Dams and flumes built on mountain streams have been
integral to the development of both foothills communi-
ties and the San Joaquin Valley below. Essentially a gravity
chute that follows a gently descending contour from a dam

to a final destination, flumes provide water for irrigation, were used to float lumber from mountain-area logging camps, and supplied water for hydraulic and placer mining operations.

The Cedars Interpretive Trail, located just outside the Bass Lake Ranger Station, explores the riparian corridor along the north fork of Willow Creek (below the Manzanita Lake dam). Despite the fact that human hands built board-walks along the trail, and a little ramshackle miner's cabin sits beside the path near the trailhead, the focus is most defi-nitely on nature. The creek is placid and slow as it meanders through willows and pines, and the pathway and boardwalks are crowded by herbs and wildflowers in season.

Cross the ranger station access road and the creek takes on a different demeanor, moving now through a narrower, tree-choked channel that lends it more speed and vigor. Mossy boulders impinge on the trail; the boardwalk winds artfully through the obstacle. The creek and trail feel remote even as they near Road 225. An overlook platform is at trail's end, where you can enjoy the creek's gentle rumble before retracing your steps toward the trailhead.

Take a final detour just before the track climbs back to the ranger station lot, walking farther upstream on a trail extension to a quiet picnic area on the bank of the creek. A little meadow, crowded with wildflowers in season, borders the area. From there, backtrack to the trailhead.

Miles and Directions

Manzanita Lake Flume
- **0.0** Start by passing the gate at the far end of the picnic area parking lot. In less than 500 feet, another road intersects; stay left on the lakeside path.

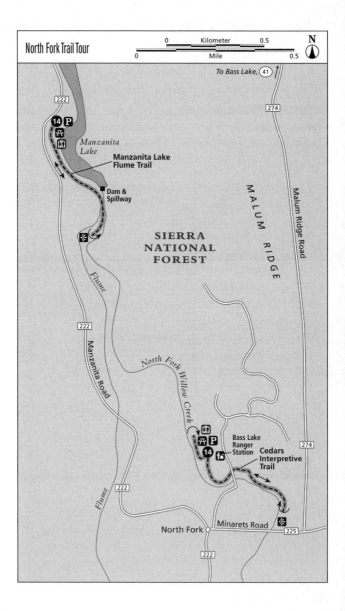

0.3 Reach the dam and enjoy the spill into Willow Creek. Pick up the low road to continue.

0.4 Arrive at the mouth of the flume. Metal grates with railings lead down to the channel's side, where you can better observe the flow. Retrace your steps from here.

0.8 Arrive back at the trailhead.

Cedars Interpretive Trail

0.0 Start at the signed trailhead in the northwest corner of the Bass Lake Ranger Station parking area. Switchbacks lead down past the little miner's cabin. After about 350 feet reach a trail junction and go straight (left), heading downstream on the path that alternates between dirt, patches of pavement, and boardwalk.

0.2 Cross the ranger station access road. The trail resumes as a boardwalk on the far side.

0.5 Reach the viewing platform overlooking the creek. This is the turnaround point; retrace your steps toward the trailhead.

1.0 Arrive back at the trail Y below the switchbacks that lead up to the ranger station. Stay left on the streamside pathway.

1.1 Reach the picnic area. Take a break, then retrace your steps.

1.2 Arrive back at the trailhead.

15 Edison Point Loop at Pine Flat Lake

Sprawling views of Pine Flat Lake, sloping meadows thick with wildflowers in season, and patches of shady oak woodland are found along the trail at Edison Point.

Distance: 2.4-mile loop
Approximate hiking time: 1.5 hours
Difficulty: Moderate due to elevation change
Trail surface: Dirt access road and dirt singletrack
Best seasons: Fall, winter, spring
Other trail users: Mountain bikers
Canine compatibility: Leashed dogs permitted

Fees and permits: None
Schedule: Open daily year-round
Trailhead facilities: Gravel parking lot, information signboard
Maps: USGS Pine Flat Dam CA
Trail contact: US Army Corps of Engineers, P.O. Box 117/27295 Pine Flat Rd., Sanger 93649-0117; (559) 787-2589; www .spk.usace.army.mil/organiza tions/cespk-co/lakes/pineflat .html

Finding the trailhead: From Fresno, head east on CA 180. Take the Fowler Avenue exit. Go 1 block south on Fowler Avenue to Belmont Avenue. Turn left, and follow Belmont Avenue east out of town; it becomes Trimmer Springs Road as you arc northeast toward the foothills. Continue on Trimmer Springs Road, past the turnoff for the hamlet of Piedra, to the junction with Pine Flat Road at about 20 miles. Stay left on Trimmer Springs Road (a right turn takes you to the dam, which is not open to the public, and to lake headquarters, which is open). Follow Trimmer Springs Road another 9.0 miles to the signed trailhead parking area on the right. GPS: N36 52.220'/W119 17.127'

The Hike

Pine Flat Lake is the upshot of an Army Corps of Engineers dam project on the Kings River that controls floodwaters downstream, provides hydroelectric power, and offers locals and visitors a place to play in the scenic foothills between Fresno and Sequoia National Park.

The dam, completed in 1954 and off-limits to the public except for guided tours, is an imposing 429-foot concrete wall. Behind the dam up to a million acre-feet of water can be impounded (enough to cover a million acres to a depth of 1 foot), creating a lake with a wide-open surface and arms that snake into forested canyons.

While four recreation areas, with campsites, boat ramps, and other amenities, are stationed along the lakeshore, there are limited hiking options with easy public access. Fortunately, the trail loop on Edison Point offers vistas and terrain sure to satisfy anyone who wants to explore on land rather than on the water.

The loop can be traveled in either direction but is described clockwise here, beginning on a gently ascending dirt road. A trail post marks the spot. The second trailhead, located to the right as you face the hillside, marks the end of the loop.

The road climbs easily under the shade of oaks and a set of power lines. Round the first big curve and the lake views open. Much of the trail, from this point on, traverses the steep, grassy hillsides, with the views alternating from east to west across the lake and into the mountains that surround it.

The road climbs to a power-line tower; here a trail sign points right and downhill. Follow the singletrack sharply downhill, then begin a more gentle switchbacking drop to a trail junction. Going left leads to a dead end in the shade, with filtered views of the lake. Go right to continue the loop, crossing another section of grassy hillside to an oak-shaded bench that overlooks the lake. Depending on lake level and season, you can pick your way down to the shoreline to wet your feet.

To continue, follow the singletrack, sometimes overgrown (especially in spring, when the grasses and wildflowers explode) but never hard to follow, on a gentle traverse through the grasses just above the shoreline. To get back to the trailhead, you'll have to climb switchbacks, but they are shaded and the grade is never extreme. Close the loop at the second trailhead at the parking area.

Miles and Directions

0.0 Start at the upper trailhead, to the left as you face the hillside. Begin climbing on the dirt access road, which curves onto an open south-facing exposure with lake views.

0.4 Arrive at the end of the road beneath a power-line tower. Good views open from the saddle, looking east across the lake. Take the signed trail that heads right (south and downhill). At the trail Y 200 feet beyond the tower, stay left and downhill.

0.6 The trail makes a sharp right-hand turn and plunges steeply downhill. Where a side trail joins, stay left and down.

0.75 Round a switchback and begin mellow traverses across the grassy hillside, enjoying the lake views.

0.8 Round another switchback.

1.1 The trail splits. The left track leads to a shady overlook. Check it out, then return to the Y and go left, traversing above a little cove.

1.4 Arrive at the bench overlooking the lake. After you've rested, pick up the trail to the left above the bench, continuing on

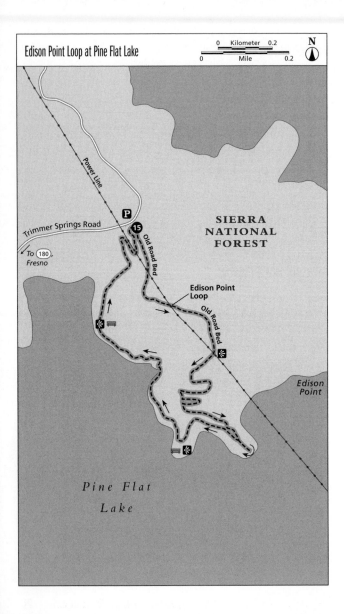

a traverse just above the shore. A series of shaded gullies breaks up the grassland.

1.9 Round the first switchback as you begin to climb back toward the trailhead.

2.0 Pass a bench at the next switchback; a little rock alcove in the hillside is just above.

2.4 Round the final switchback and arrive back at the trailhead.

16 Kaweah Oaks Preserve

Tucked off a country road south of Fresno, trails in this little preserve wind through valley oak woodlands to thickets of wild grape and wild rose watered by a confluence of ditches, Deep Creek, and an unusual old sycamore tree.

Distance: 4.1 miles in four loops with connector trail
Approximate hiking time: 2 hours
Difficulty: Easy
Trail surface: Dirt road, dirt singletrack
Best seasons: Year-round
Other trail users: None
Canine compatibility: Dogs not permitted
Fees and permits: None
Schedule: Open daily year-round. Hours change with the seasons: winter, 8 a.m. to 5 p.m.; spring and fall, 8 a.m. to 6 p.m.; summer, 8 a.m. to 7 p.m.
Trailhead facilities: Gravel parking lot, gateway pavilion

with information signboards and benches. Water is available at the picnic site.
Maps: USGS Exeter CA; posted on the information signboard in the gateway pavilion
Other: Trail interpretive guides are available through the Sequoia Riverlands Trust office. A small donation is requested. They may also be in the map box on site. Return the guide for the next trail user.
Trail contact: Sequoia River-lands Trust, 427 S. Garden St., Visalia 93277; (559) 738-0211; www.sequoiariverlands.org

Finding the trailhead: From Fresno, head south on CA 99 to Visalia. Take the exit for CA 198 and go east about 13 miles to the junction with Road 182. A little brown sign with a hiker icon precedes the junction. Turn left onto Road 182 and go 0.5 mile to the signed trailhead on the left. GPS: N36 20.027' / W119 10.003'

The Hike

Four short trail loops explore the native valley oak woodland of this 322-acre nature preserve. Protected with the help of the Nature Conservancy back in 1983, Kaweah Oaks is a time capsule containing a pocket of the environment similar to that inhabited by California natives before the arrival of European settlers.

The names of the four short loops that branch off from the main access trail (a wide dirt road) give away the native features they showcase. On the Grapevine Trail wild grapes create bowers over the path. Wild rose weaves through the undergrowth on the Wild Rose Trail. In wet years a swamp/pond forms along the Swamp Trail. And one of the highlights of the Sycamore Trail is an old sycamore with a trunk that runs parallel to the ground and boughs that reach skyward.

But there's much more to see along the loops than just the namesake features. Both the Wild Rose and Grapevine Trails wind through a lush riparian zone shaded by cottonwood and willow, with thickets of wildflowers and wild herbs encroaching on the paths, especially in spring. Bridges cross the intersecting irrigation ditches at the mouths of the trails; depending on the flows, these can be rushing, with whitewater spilling through the funnels, or placid and low.

Deep Creek winds along the backside of the Swamp Trail—a lazy stream with a grassy, shaded bank that invites you to linger. An ephemeral pond appears when the rains have been ample and the water table is high; look for (but do not disturb) the pond turtles that live here.

The Sycamore Trail is the sleeper among the loops. It starts in pastureland, then plunges through thickets of blackberry and little meadows choked with annual grasses. Benches provide opportunities to sit and listen to the birds that rumble through the hedges of berry bushes that line the path. The namesake sycamore has to be seen to be believed: Its huge trunk stretches along the ground, while limbs as thick as trees shoot upward into the canopy.

All four trails are interpretive and lined with numbered trail posts. Though boxes for guides are at the trailhead, there's no guarantee one will be available when you visit. Contact the trust to obtain a copy.

You can explore all or part of the preserve, taking the trails in any order you wish. A broad dirt road links the well-signed options, winding through the alkali meadow at the heart of the preserve. Parts of the meadow are open to grazing, so expect to find cattle alongside (and sometimes standing on) the roadway. They are gentle, wary creatures, and will move out of your way. You should also expect road noise on some of the paths, as CA 198 is just beyond the cottonwoods to the south of the preserve.

The route described in the Miles and Directions section encompasses all four trails, beginning with the Grapevine and Wild Rose loops, moving on to the Swamp Trail, and finishing with the Sycamore Trail.

Miles and Directions

0.0 Start by passing through the gateway pavilion and the gate that leads onto the dirt road.

0.1 Pass porta-potties and a gate, staying on the wide dirt track.

0.25 Pass a picnic area behind a gate, then the signed junction with the Sycamore Trail, on the right. Again, stay on the roadway and be sure to close the gate behind you.

0.5 Arrive at the junction of the access trail with the Grapevine, Wild Rose, and Swamp Trails. Go left, over the bridge that spans the ditch, to the Grapevine and Wild Rose Trails. Cross a second bridge to the left, over the ditch diversion dam, to the start of the signed Grapevine Trail. Go left again, and over another little bridge.

0.6 The trail splits; go right to continue the clockwise loop.

0.8 Close the loop and backtrack to the start of the Wild Rose Trail. Trail marker 1 is beside the ditch at a picnic table. The loop begins at marker 2; go left to travel in a clockwise direction.

1.1 Close the Wild Rose loop and backtrack to the Swamp Trail sign. Pick up the dirt road to the left, heading west through the meadow.

1.4 Arrive at the start of the signed Swamp Trail loop. Go right on the singletrack. The loop trail segments merge in about 100 yards; go right to travel the loop in a counterclockwise direction.

1.5 Reach a gate and a Swamp Trail sign. Follow the path through mown grass into the woodlands that shelter Deep Creek.

1.8 Arrive at the banks of Deep Creek. The trail bends left and follows the creek for a stretch before turning back toward the meadow.

2.2 Close the loop. Retrace your steps back up to the main dirt track and go left, backtracking to the Sycamore Trail junction.

2.7 Pass the gate and arrive at the Sycamore Trail intersection. Go left on the Sycamore Trail. This is where the cows live, along with their cow pies. Watch your step.

3.0 Arrive at a gate and the start of the Sycamore loop. Pass through the break in the fence and go right along the fence to the trail sign. Start to the left, following the loop in a clockwise direction.

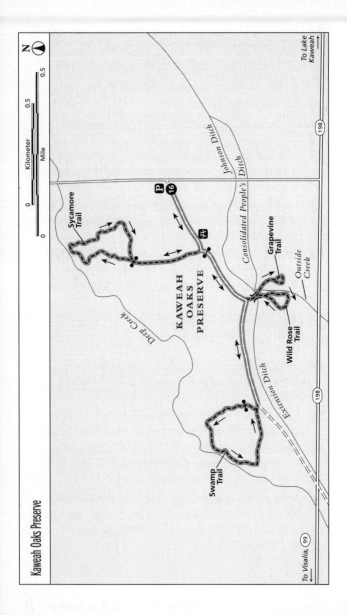

Kaweah Oaks Preserve

3.2 Pass a few benches facing the blackberry thickets. Just beyond, the trail bends close to Deep Creek.

3.4 Arrive at the sycamore. Go left past the tree to continue.

3.6 Head through a bower of grapevines, limbo under willow limbs to the fence line, and close the loop. Retrace your steps to the start of the Sycamore Trail, then go left to backtrack to the trailhead.

4.1 Arrive back at the trailhead.

17 San Luis National Wildlife Refuge

Tour San Joaquin River marshlands flush with birdlife on two loops that pass through an area that hearkens back to what California's Great Valley looked like before the river was dammed and channeled.

Distance: 3.1-mile double loop
Approximate hiking time: 2 hours
Difficulty: Easy
Trail surface: Gravel roadway, dirt singletrack, mowed grass
Best seasons: Fall, winter, spring
Other trail users: None
Canine compatibility: Leashed dogs permitted
Fees and permits: None
Schedule: Open daily year-round from one-half hour before sunrise to one-half hour after sunset
Trailhead facilities: Small gravel parking area, restrooms, interpretive kiosk. Additional parking is available at the wildlife refuge's West Bear Creek Unit entrance, along with an information signboard.

Maps: USGS Stevinson CA; online at www.fws.gov/sanluis/ Maps/West%20Bear%20 Creek%20Unit%20Map.pdf
Special considerations: Portions of the national wildlife refuge are open to waterfowl hunting in season (usually from mid-Oct to Jan). No hunting occurs on nature trails or auto tour routes. Contact the refuge managers for more information or visit the website. Also, given the marshy nature of the area, insects can by pesky. Wear long pants and a long-sleeved shirt or use bug repellent.
Trail contact: San Luis National Wildlife Refuge Complex, P.O. Box 2176, Los Banos 93635; (209) 826-3508; www.fws.gov/ sanluis

Finding the trailhead: From Fresno, take CA 99 north for about 55 miles to Merced. Take the exit for CA 140 (Yosemite Parkway).

Go left onto 14th Street and follow 14th Street to V Street. Turn left on V Street, pass under the CA 99 freeway, and join CA 140 heading west. Follow CA 140 west for about 20 miles to its junction with CA 165. Turn left on CA 165 and drive 3.2 miles, crossing the San Joaquin River, to the signed West Bear Creek Unit entrance on the left. Follow the one-way auto tour route (a gravel road) for about 1 mile to the signed access road for the trailhead parking area on the right. GPS: N37 16.604'/W120 50.758'

The Hike

Though it takes more than an hour to reach the San Luis National Wildlife Refuge from Fresno, it's included in this guide for one overriding reason. The terrain traveled on these two loops is about as close as you'll come to seeing the flatlands of the San Joaquin Valley as they were before the rivers were dammed, the canals were built, and the ground was plowed and planted and parceled out as range.

This unique ecological complex, which also encompasses Great Valley Grasslands State Park (an undeveloped park property), is hardly pristine. CA 165, a sometimes-busy two-lane highway, bisects the area, and the grasslands are crisscrossed by farm, levee, and hunting access roads. But since coming under federal protection and the implementation of restoration efforts, the abundance of birdlife and plant life now thriving in the San Joaquin's bottomlands is akin to that which naturalist John Muir waxed poetic about in the late 1800s.

The stats of the national wildlife refuge are impressive. Encompassing more than 26,600 acres and comprising separate units, the refuge protects thriving riparian zones, parcels of native grassland, and vernal pools. Located on the Pacific Flyway, migratory waterfowl and shorebirds flock to the area, including many species of duck (which are targeted by hunters in season). Insects and mammals, including the endangered tiger salamander and San Joaquin kit fox, as well as the once nearly extinct tule elk, find sanctuary here.

This route connects the Raccoon Marsh and Woody Pond nature trail loops. Both are described in a counterclockwise direction, beginning with the Woody Pond Trail, but you can combine the loops as suits your needs. Begin by following a mown doubletrack along a slough overgrown with thick grass, wildflowers, and riparian trees such as cottonwood and willow. At the trail junction at the ditch gate, go right, over the ditch, and follow signs onto the levee road that serves as the outward leg of the Woody Pond Trail. Trail signs keep you on track.

The Woody Pond Trail loops around a vernal pool at its northern reach, and returns toward the trailhead via a mown singletrack that skirts the thickly wooded shores of the namesake pond. Close the loop at the slough bridge, cross back over the slough to the signed start of the Raccoon Marsh Trail, and head north on the mown track that borders a bird-filled marshland on the left. The latter part of the Raccoon Marsh track is wedged between the marsh and CA 165, but it's still an enjoyable walk, especially if you are a birder. The trail ends on the auto tour roadway; turn left and follow the road back to the trailhead.

Miles and Directions

0.0 Start on the signed trail behind the restroom building.

0.1 At the trail junction at the ditch gate, go right, across the ditch, on the Woody Pond Trail (the Raccoon Marsh Trail is left/straight ahead).

0.2 Signs point the way over the slough bridge and onto the levee road that serves as the Woody Pond Trail. Go left on the broad, straight roadway, with bird-filled bottomland marshes on both sides.

0.9 Just as the trail begins to bend west toward the highway, a sign points you down and left onto the mown path. Skirt the edge of a pond created by water that backs up behind the slough gate, heading toward the thick stands of trees that grow on the banks of Woody Pond.

1.3 Pass trail signs that direct you along the path, which is briefly wedged between the pond and the highway, with the pond on the left.

1.4 Water lies on both sides of the trail as you pass through a rehabilitated area.

1.7 Pass a nature trail sign.

1.9 Close the loop at the bridge over the slough. Go right over the bridge, then right again on the Raccoon Marsh Trail. Follow the mown grass path alongside the marsh, with views of the distant Coast Range to the west visible on clear days.

2.1 Pass a nature trail sign. Wild fennel, smelling faintly of licorice, grows in dense stands along the right side of the trail.

2.8 Bump up against the highway, with nature trail and exit signs pointing you down the path that bends left and runs between the edge of the marsh and the roadway.

3.0 The Raccoon Marsh Trail ends on the auto tour road. Go left on the road and follow it back to the parking area, which is in sight.

3.1 Arrive back at the trailhead.

Options: A number of hiking options are available in the grasslands complex, which includes the nearby Merced and Kesterson units. The San Joaquin River National Wildlife Refuge near Modesto has a 3.8-mile nature trail that explores restored seasonal marshland and old–growth valley oak woodlands. Neighboring Great Valley Grasslands State

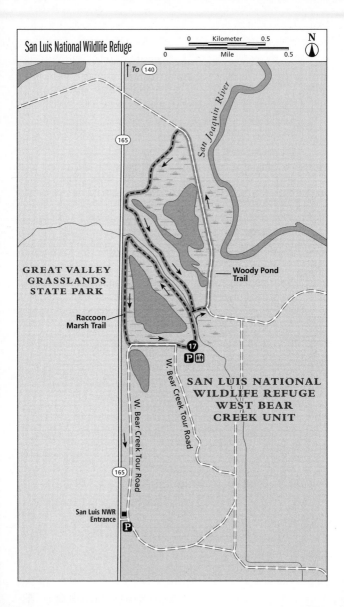

Park offers a 6.0-mile tour of the San Joaquin bottomlands, but does not (as of 2011) offer a formal trailhead or any amenities. The San Luis NWR website outlines options and provides maps; the Great Valley Grasslands site, where the day hike option is described but not mapped, is available at www.parks.ca.gov.

Day Hikes Gear List

- ❏ camera/film/extra batteries
- ❏ compass/GPS unit
- ❏ pedometer
- ❏ daypack
- ❏ first-aid kit
- ❏ food
- ❏ guidebook
- ❏ headlamp/flashlight with extra batteries and bulbs
- ❏ hat
- ❏ insect repellent
- ❏ knife/multipurpose tool
- ❏ map
- ❏ matches and fire starter in waterproof container
- ❏ fleece jacket
- ❏ rain gear
- ❏ space blanket
- ❏ sunglasses
- ❏ sunscreen
- ❏ watch
- ❏ water
- ❏ water bottles/hydration system

About the Author

Tracy Salcedo-Chourré has written more than twenty-five guidebooks to destinations in California and Colorado, including *Hiking Lassen Volcanic National Park*, *A FalconGuide to California's Missions and Presidios*, *Exploring Point Reyes National Seashore and the Golden Gate National Recreation Area*, *Best Rail Trails California*, and Best Easy Day Hikes guides to Boulder, Denver, Aspen, Colorado Springs, San Francisco's Peninsula, San Francisco's East Bay, San Francisco's North Bay, San Jose, Lake Tahoe, Reno, and Sacramento.

She is also an editor, teacher, and mom—but somehow still finds time to hike, swim, and garden. She lives with her husband, three sons, and a small menagerie of pets in California's Wine Country.

What's So Special about Unspoiled, Natural Places?

Beauty   Solitude   Wildness   Freedom   Quiet   Adventure
Serenity   Inspiration   Wonder   Excitement
Relaxation   Challenge

There's a lot to love about our treasured public lands, and the reasons are different for each of us. Whatever your reasons are, the national **Leave No Trace** education program will help you discover special outdoor places, enjoy them, and preserve them—today and for those who follow. By practicing and passing along these simple principles, you can help protect the special places you love from being loved to death.

The Principles of Leave No Trace

- Plan ahead and prepare
- Travel and camp on durable surfaces
- Dispose of waste properly
- Leave what you find
- Minimize campfire impacts
- Respect wildlife
- Be considerate of other visitors

Leave No Trace is a national nonprofit organization dedicated to teaching responsible outdoor recreation skills and ethics to everyone who enjoys spending time outdoors.

To learn more or to become a member, please visit us at www.LNT.org or call (800) 332-4100.

Leave No Trace, P.O. Box 997, Boulder, CO 80306